Non-Violence and Ecological Imperatives

Non-Violence and Ecological Imperatives: A Nature's Call

Professor Ramin Jahanbegloo and Dr. Pooja Sharma

ANTHEM PRESS

Anthem Press
An imprint of Wimbledon Publishing Company
www.anthempress.com

This edition first published in UK and USA 2025
by ANTHEM PRESS
75–76 Blackfriars Road, London SE1 8HA, UK
or PO Box 9779, London SW19 7ZG, UK
and
244 Madison Ave #116, New York, NY 10016, USA

British Library Cataloguing-in-Publication Data
A catalogue record for this book is available from the British Library.

Library of Congress Cataloging-in-Publication Data: 2025933786
A catalog record for this book has been requested.

ISBN-13: 978-1-83999-330-5 (Hbk)
ISBN-10: 1-83999-330-8 (Hbk)

Cover Credit: Professor Ramin Jahanbegloo

This title is also available as an e-book.

Dedicated
To
"The Animals of Our Planet"

Humanity will learn the true meaning of life the day we acknowledge the message of unconditional love that animals teach us. Biologically, animals may deal with conflicts among themselves, but only they know what the true meaning of tolerance is and what respecting each other's space and boundary means. Today, humans need to learn several attributes from animals: selfless love, surrender, forgiveness, and so on. Every animal and each species in the jungle leaves a deep lesson for the life of humankind. The leopard conveys the profound message of patience, the ants demonstrate cooperation and teamwork, and the virtue of a simple and peaceful life shown by the deer can never be ignored while seeking the fundamental values in life. The respect for hierarchy reflected by elephants, the lion's strength and courage, the loyalty of a dog, and a spider's perseverance and diligence convey the lesson of consistent hard work.

Thus, the biggest tribute humankind can ever offer to green non-violence is to love and preserve the animals around us. Loving animals and caring for them is the most non-violent and harmonious act humans can perform in the present times. The attribute of compassion towards animals is the greatest virtue we can manifest as a non-violent response to a plea for Nature. By dedicating this book to all the animals on planet Earth, we express our deep remorse for the unprecedented anguish caused to the animal kingdom by the brutal and barbarous acts of humankind. Our little gesture of kindness and compassion towards animals can forgive our sins and make us a little more humane.

CONTENTS

INTRODUCTION: GREEN NON-VIOLENCE

Man is the only living being who kills, destroys, and conquers for power, pleasure, and greed. According to Schopenhauer, "Man is the only animal who causes pain to others with no other object than wanting to do so."[1] And it is precisely this capacity for deeds of violence which has separated humankind from the natural world. As such, human civilisation has been advancing with this dual capacity of asserting love, compassion, and creativity, while being the cause of the greatest evils of history. From 5000 BCE (the rise of Sumer) until today, humans have shown a great capacity for violence, depravity, and cruelty. Yet, all through history, the primary object of this extreme violence has been Nature and its vital elements. The agony of being unable to answer the question, why mankind conquered and destroyed Nature the way it did, has been the burden of modern civilisation. As a matter of fact, modern Man betrayed the universally accepted ideals of life and biodiversity, that is, harmony, coexistence, and pluralism, by replacing them with selfishness, greed, and hostility. And now, on the 25th hour of its destructive existence, mankind has realised that the price of human progress has been nothing but death and destruction for the mountains, skies, oceans, lakes, rivers, forests, and animals. As a general rule, it can be said that human beings have become Nature's enemy No.1. No living being is safe as long as the human race exists. As the famous Stoic philosopher, Marcus Aurelius, observed: "The earth [...], though so grievously abused, still suffers me to tread its surface."[2] All of this implies that the human being is a strange mixture of creativity and monstrosity. In the words of Pascal, "What a chimera is man! What a novelty, a monster, a chaos, a contradiction, a prodigy! Judge of all things, an imbecile worm; depository of truth, and sewer of error and doubt; the glory and refuse

1 Schopenhauer, Arthur, *Essays and Aphorisms*, translated by R.J. Hollingdale, London: Penguin Books, 2004, p. 139.

2 Marcus Aurelius, *Meditations*, Book V/4, London: Penguin Books, 2004, p. 44.

of the universe."[3] That is, Man's metaphysical dimension still reflects a capacity to be either the destroyer of worlds or a cosmic companion of the universe. Of course, if we consider ourselves as the inhabitants of a World House, our survival depends alarmingly on a non-violent philosophy of life.

The non-violent philosophy of life is a non-reductionist attitude of life, revolving around the concept of epistemic humility. It is on the basis of this epistemic humility that we need to establish today's ecological imperatives. As such, a non-violent attitude towards the biosphere in particular, and the concept of life in general, is primarily an act of maturity. We do not become fully mature until we learn how to live humbly in the world and share it with other living beings. Therefore, non-violence is a completeness of life through the development of a dialogical maturity in mankind. The day humanity learns to have a dialogue with Nature, it will also renew its ecological commitments to the idea of non-violence. This is only possible if mankind accepts the truth that the spirit of the earth is ailing because the principle of life has been brutalized.

In the *Visions Seminars* that he gave in the 1930s, Carl Gustav Jung declared: "The earth has a spirit of her own, a beauty of her own."[4] Undoubtedly, Jung's main plea for Nature was to insist on its original wholeness. From Jung's point of view, our loss of connection with the planet Earth was neither an ethical nor a psychological problem, but a spiritual one. Three chapters of this book have been devoted to three important figures with a spiritual approach to Nature: Henry David Thoreau, Mahatma Gandhi, and Rabindranath Tagore. Hence it follows that the utmost power of Nature can only be given in a spiritual context capable of opening our eyes and bringing light to them. From this, we may gather that life is something much more important than our daily habits. Like Thoreau and Tagore, Jung also believed that Nature could talk to us. He wrote in a letter to a colleague in 1947: "Why not go into the forest for a time, literally? Sometimes a tree tells you more than can be read in books."[5] Jung's concern over Man's loss of connection with Nature is ours today, but this cannot be taught to the next generations if we do not consider the Earth as our mother. It's only when we feel this kinship with the Earth that we will be able to feel its suffering and witness its destruction. Our life is governed today by ecological imperatives that govern every angle of our existence as a living being. The choice before us is no longer loving or not

3 Pascal, Blaise, *Pensées*, New York: E.P. Dutton & Co., 1958, p. 121.

4 Jung, Carl Gustav, *The Visions Seminars*, Zurich: Spring Publications, 1976, pp. 133–134.

5 Jung, Carl Gustav, *Letters*, Vol. 1, edited by G. Adler, Princeton: Princeton University Press, 1975, p. 479.

loving the Earth. It's saving the Earth or the non-existence of humanity. But the Earth cannot be saved by politics and politicians. It can only be saved by a new human approach to life, a new philosophy of existence. It means not only striving to be non-violent to the environment and to all other living beings around us but also trying to be non-violent to ourselves and to those around us. A culture of green non-violence is not an impossible dream, since it is a plea for Nature and a necessary leap for the future of mankind. Until now, we looked at the planet Earth as a luxury. Today, its survival has become a necessity. Green non-violence is the consciousness of this necessity.

A plea for Nature starts here and now with an act of green non-violence. As such, the first statement on the defence of Nature and Mother Earth is the history of non-violence itself. We should not forget that oriental religions like Jainism, Hinduism, Buddhism, and Zoroastrianism were fundamentally spiritual pillars of non-violent and ecological attitudes towards life. All these four oriental religions emphasise the ethics of non-injury and kindness to all living beings and are committed to certain virtues like humility, compassion, and respect. As such, they all anticipated the contemporary wisdom of green non-violence. If we take the example of Buddhism, we can say that the environmental implications of a virtue like compassion are most evident, both in the teachings of Buddhism and in the lives of Indian or Tibetan Buddhists. "One of the most important figures in this regard is surely Asoka, the 3rd century BCE king, whose realm extended over most of modern India. Profoundly affected by the teaching of *ahimsa*, Asoka instituted a number of 'environmental' measures, including the banning of animal sacrifices, the protection of various non-food animals and birds, the institution of vegetarianism at court, the planting of trees, restrictions on the burning of forests, and the creation of fifty-six 'no slaughter' days per year."[6] Let us not forget that all major religions of the East share the belief that the experience of *ahimsa* (non-violence) is the only way to find harmony and peace within the universe. Thus, there is a shared commitment to *ahimsa* which needs to be stressed in everyday life and Man's encounter with Nature, so that our self-centred attitudes are replaced by the idea of interdependence in the world. The Buddha established the Four Noble Truths and insisted on the centrality and importance of the renunciation of ill-will and the development of harmlessness. We can, therefore, understand the significance of ahimsa as green non-violence and the commitment to achieve personal enlightenment while having a harmonious and harmless attitude towards the world.

---

6 David, E., James, Simon P., *Buddhism, Virtue and Environment*, London: Routledge, 2017, p. 136.

> The purpose is to recognize our interdependence as sentient beings who suffer due to the three qualities of existence: impermanence, dissatisfaction (suffering) and no-self. After realizing that we share the same existence and that this relative reality is contingent on our thoughts and actions, the Buddha taught ways to change unwholesome states of mind and actions to wholesome ones which will lead us to the Supreme Enlightenment [...]. Therefore, it is not about the quest for individual Enlightenment only to save oneself from the *samsaric* existence but is rather about an individual and social commitment to reach the shores of *Nirvana* through compassionate actions rooted in the belief in interdependence and the mutual right to overcome suffering.[7]

Following this vision, human beings can work towards a harmonic exchange with Nature. Therefore, green non-violence is an everyday practice where one becomes part of Nature and the universe in every thought and action and towards all sentient beings. According to David Kaczynski, "as Buddhists, we also understand that there is no truth or wisdom without compassion. Engaged Buddhism represents an antidote to the politics of fear, hate, violence, and separation."[8] The harmonic exchange binds us with all living beings, who despite biological differences share the same *samsaric* existence and the mutual need to overcome suffering. This connection is constructed with wholesome non-violence—universal and cosmic—which will eventually lead to the balance of the world. What humanity can learn from the harmonic exchange between humankind and Nature is the idea of achieving non-violent coexistence and universal balance. When this is done, there will be no room for rational reductionism, epistemological arrogance, and the conquest of Nature. The interdependent comprehension of reality opens the door to a true communion with the universe, reflecting the transcendent and compassionate nature of green non-violence. In the words of the Buddha, "Just as that great cloud, raining on all the plants, trees, thickets, forests, and medicinal herbs, and according to the nature of their seed perfectly fertilizing them so that each grows and develops, [so] the Law preached by the Tathagata is of one form and flavor, that is to say, deliverance, abandonment, extinction, and finally the attainment of perfect knowledge [...] The Tathagata knows this

7 Chavez-Segura, Alejandro, *A Theology of International Relations: A Buddhist Approach to Religion and Politics in an Interdependent World*, St. Andrews: University of St. Andrews, Dissertation, 2011, pp. 39–40

8 Kaczynski, David, "Why Democracy Needs Dharma," in *Mindful Politics: A Buddhist Guide to Making the World a Better Place*, edited by Melvin McLeod, Boston: Wisdom Publications, 2006, p. 107.

unitary essential Law, that is to say, deliverance, abandonment, extinction, final nirvana of eternal tranquility, ending in a return to the void."[9]

Gandhi believed non-violence could be put into practice at every level of human experience. Non-violence for him was not just a political tactic but spirituality and a way of life. We are living today in an era where our relations with the biosphere and environmental issues have become not only economic and political problems but also ethical and spiritual. But green non-violence still offers us an ideal that may be upheld. At a time when mankind is confronted with global warming and the destruction of biodiversity on planet Earth, green non-violence can be a well-trusted means of laying the groundwork for a new cosmic fellowship. Though many continue to believe that green non-violence is an ineffective instrument against the corporate mindset and the destruction of Nature, in the last several decades many spiritual and ethical initiatives, which were premised on non-violent philosophy and an affirmation of peaceful coexistence, helped build global civil society on solid foundations, could be associated with a kind of neo-Gandhian quest for peace and harmony with Mother Earth. Therefore, the choice of green non-violence is ours. We live in a world of overlapping destinies where the fate of the human race and that of planet Earth are heavily intertwined. Never in the history of humanity has non-violence been so crucially green and practised in the direction of Nature.

Under the framework of new cosmic fellowship, there have been several noble experiments undertaken related to green non-violence. Gandhi himself experimented with green non-violence through constructive work and initiatives. He advocated and formulated several concepts and ideologies integrating green non-violence. Gandhi used the phrase "Economy of Nature", bringing about a sensitivity and deeper understanding of human actions and ecology. The proposed cosmic fellowship is fundamentally based on the interconnectedness of humankind and nature, as advocated by Gandhi. All the constructive initiatives or programmes undertaken by Gandhi were motivated to rebuild the lost harmony between humankind and nature. The primary objective of all the movements was "freeing the world from detrimental greed of materialism". Gandhi asserted that the mindless consumption of natural resources became the reason for unsustainable modern civilization. The message conveyed through every programme or initiative was that the responsible consumption of raw materials, as a part of an ecologically oriented lifestyle and economy, reduces the risk that policies of violence will be

9 Kato, Bunno, Tamura, Yoshiro, *The Threefold Lotus Sutra*, Tokyo: Kosei Publishing, 1989, p. 128.

pursued. Under the stewardship of cosmic fellowship, ecological sustainability calls for the responsibility of human beings to maintain and preserve the interlinkages between man, nature, and other living and non-living entities.

Gandhi's remarkable notion of "Sarvodaya", implying "welfare of all", was a community-centred approach, ensuring the betterment of life. The lack of emphasis on non-use value and altruistic value, as well as missing focus on "Biocentrism", paved the way towards "Gandhian Economics" and the notion of an "Economy of Permanence". The biocentric view states that all living things must be given equal priority when it comes to ethical and moral decisions. Further, the notion of means and ends holds phenomenal significance in the goal of ecological sustainability. The interconnection between means and ends is more ethical than technical. He emphasised that evil or violent means will never lead to good ends. His notion of means and ends is similar to that of a seed and a tree, signifying the close connection between the two. He contends that the end lies in the means just as the tree lies within the seed. Gandhi himself led an essentially non-violent life, respecting nature and its creations. He advocated conscious efforts to use the resources of nature to the bare minimum in an attempt to conserve natural resources even if they are available in abundance.

For Gandhi, Nature was analogous to God. However, when Nature is not considered God and is understood as limited by Time and Space, then nature could strike through in the future. In this context, human life is said to be Transient compared to that of Nature which is Permanent.[10] This philosophy reinforces the individual to adopt a lifestyle guided by the individual responsibility that arises from the essence of the continuity of life. Gandhi believed in the oneness of life; all creation, both living and non-living, are so closely interdependent that one cannot harm the other without harming oneself. Thus, his notion was a remarkable, viable extension of "Pareto optimality", which failed to incorporate the environment in the discourse. A Pareto optimality is a state in which resources are optimised in a manner that any movement away from this state will make at least one person worse off without making any other person better off.

On the ground level, Gandhi experimented with green non-violence through the construction of ashrams, which served as laboratories of non-violence, "ahimsa", where Gandhi tested his moral and spiritual hypothesis. The journey of self-transformation, which is the underlying principle of Gandhian philosophy, travelled through both the inner and outer worlds. It was never

---

10 https://www.emerald.com/insight/content/doi/10.1108/978-1-83753-380-020231010/full/html?skipTracking=true.

independent of the community, society, and ecology around it. This journey of inner evolution towards sustainable pathways of living could practically evolve in perfectly designed ashrams that operated on Gandhian principles. The ashrams of Gandhi served as experimental laboratories for a non-violent, alternative way of living.[11] These ashrams later became the epitome of peace, harmony, self-renunciation, and constructive work. The ashrams were small communities that practiced the principles of Truth and non-violence.

Based on Ruskin's philosophy "Unto This Last", Gandhi established Phoenix Settlement in Natal and Tolstoy Farm. The underlying notion behind these settlements was that a simple life based on love, labour, and the dignity of human beings became the centre stage of all alternative ways of living. Gandhi believed that an individual's life was meant for self-realisation through experiment. Self-realisation comes from the search for Truth, more specifically the absolute Truth as ultimate reality.[12] An individual must strive to discover what truth means for him and practice it in life with single-mindedness. Truth can also be explained as "soul force". The process of self-realisation and self-transformation is a continuum process and it requires effort each day. The daily life in the ashram must reflect the new order or phenomenon necessary to realise the transformation.

Each of the residents of the ashram was consistently engaged in the act of community work and service. The residents of the ashram tilled the soil together, cooked meals together, spun the clothes together, and cleaned the toilets, breaking all the barriers of caste, gender, race, and religion. They practiced non-violence and harmony all the time and inculcated the moral pursuit of truth, satyagraha. The ashrams reflected a consolidated community demonstrating complete civic responsibility.

The first ashram in India was established at Kochrab village in Paldi near Ahmedabad in 1915 after he returned from South Africa. The Satyagraha Ashram at Kochrab in 1915 was shifted to Sabarmati Ashram located on the banks of the river Sabarmati in 1917. In Sabarmati Ashram, Gandhi embarked on several experiments such as spinning and weaving, and khadi evolved as a symbol of economic liberation. The ashram life was very busy and engaging; everyone was assigned some duty and responsibility. Every person needed to exert some manual work. The ashram had a spinning and weaving department, a cowshed and a large farm. The individuals living in the ashram cleaned their plates and washed their clothes. There was no

11 https://egyankosh.ac.in/bitstream/123456789/63923/1/Block-4.pdf.

12 https://www.mkgandhi.org/articles/surendrabhana.php#:~:text=The%20Tolstoy%20Farm%20was%20the,the%20dignity%20of%20human%20beings.

concept of servants in the ashram. As khadi became the symbol of national integration and freedom, the ashram adopted khadi as their forefront work. Many of the women were untouchables, and they were encouraged to join the spinning and weaving work.

In 1934, Gandhi selected Wardha for Harijan service and the promotion of village industries. In the Wardha Ashram, fellow inmates were motivated to take up village work, on the same lines as the Sabarmati Ashram. The kitchen, toilets, and premises of the ashram were kept absolutely spotless, while the residents cleaned and washed their utensils. Some of the daily activities were compulsory, such as daily cleaning of the teeth with neem or babul twigs. The ashram began to provide mass employment to various sections of society, even in the surrounding villages. Various cooperative organizations emerged, such as "Charkha Parishramalaya" (spinning wheel work centre), established to popularise khadi in the village. The main task of individuals associated with these initiatives was to promote handmade products in place of factory products. For instance, khadi instead of mill cloth, village earthen pots instead of factory-made china, reed pens instead of steel pens, handmade paper instead of ordinary paper, babul twigs instead of toothbrushes, ordinary village jaggery instead of factory sugar, and hand-pounded whole rice instead of mill-polished rice.

Among the diverse groups of people, a large section of India lives near nature. The tribal societies belonging to remote areas represent an ethnic base of Indigenous communities with their unique pattern of living, originating from nature. The tribal communities play an instrumental role in demonstrating green non-violence in a similar way to the Gandhian ashram. The Gandhian ashrams were man-made, designed to experiment with the relationship between man and man and also between man and nature. However, the tribal communities share an ancient tradition of harmony between man and nature, well embedded in their culture. The Indigenous knowledge of tribal communities and their best practices to live in harmony with nature have enabled them to predict nature and disasters related to nature to a very large extent. They are able to predict the probability of occurrence of drought or flood calamities. Some ancient Hindu sutras predict monsoons and inform people about the potential yield of agriculture. Medicinal plants and livelihood are other aspects that are significantly addressed by the traditional knowledge system of tribal, rural, and remote areas.

The remarkable symbiosis between traditional ecological knowledge, traditional and religious practices, and the belief system is an outcome of the philosophical evolution of tribal communities. In the man–nature relationship sphere, the natural universe is constantly a part of the relationship between man and nature. Under the man-to-man relationships, the relationships are confined to their tribal world. All human beings are believed to be active and do not seek any stratification. The tribal communities in this region have inherently adopted traditional methods of conserving social, cultural, and biological resources. They have designed effective devices and strategies for the conservation of natural resources.[13] The tribals have developed a symbiotic relationship between endowed biological resources and cultural diversities. The role of tribals in preventing the loss of biodiversity is of great significance. Their traditional knowledge of preserving the useful species of medicinal plants and vegetables is the most sustainable solution in the present times. Most of the tribal communities adopt the consensus-based, participatory model of governance where each member of the community has the complete right or voice in the decision-making of the community.

13 Lal, C., Prasher, R.S. "Traditional Knowledge Systems and Conservation Practices in Tribal Society of Western Himalayas: A Case Study of District Kinnaur of Himachal Pradesh," *International Journal of Farm Sciences*, 2016, 6(3), pp. 159–171.

Part I

THEORIES OF ECOLOGICAL NON-VIOLENCE

Chapter 1

HENRY DAVID THOREAU: FREEDOM IN THE WILDERNESS

Henry David Thoreau is the greatest ecological thinker, and one of the most original and compelling writers on Nature in the English language. As a matter of fact, Thoreau's spiritual and philosophical approach to wilderness shaped an ideal that influenced American ecological thinking for over a century. This ideal had some moral force, which marked a highly articulate account of the relationship between human beings and the wilderness. Thoreau's classical piece of literature entitled *Walden* (1854) detailed his own experience of leaving society and living in the woods for two years. In the finest Romantic tradition, Thoreau showed his readers how his meaningful life in Nature brought him close to elements of Eastern mysticism and Western transcendence. Thoreau's growing knowledge about Nature and its ecological imperatives helped him to review the concepts of State and society in his time. Turning the muted voices of Nature into experiences of dissidence, Thoreau abandoned the Romantic idea of Nature and Life, while apprehending and displaying a multifaceted Truth. Thoreau did not approach Nature as an impersonal entity. On the contrary, he believed that one can listen to and learn from Nature if one enables its higher types of spiritual powers. Thoreau had no doubt that human beings needed to appreciate and sympathise with Nature. Thoreau knew that if human beings became aware of their inner spiritual forces, they could attain new perspectives in life and communicate with Nature. He saw this dialogue with nature as a path to joyousness and exultation. In *Walden*, Thoreau instructs us:

> If the day and the night are such that you greet them with joy, and life emits a fragrance like flowers and sweet-scented herbs, is more elastic, more starry, more immortal—that is your success. All nature is your congratulation, and you have cause momentarily to bless yourself. The greatest gains and values are farthest from being appreciated. We easily come to doubt if they exist. We soon forget them. They are the highest reality. Perhaps the facts most astounding and most real are

> never communicated by man to man. The true harvest of my daily life is somewhat as intangible and indescribable as the tints of morning or evening. It is a little stardust caught, a segment of the rainbow which I have clutched.[1]

Walden represents a touchstone for anyone who is in search of cosmic friendship and a spiritual journey into the eternal mystery of Being. Accordingly, for Thoreau, going to the Walden Pond was a process of Socratic self-examination. Like Socrates, Thoreau came to the conclusion that every individual had full knowledge of the higher law by addressing his/her soul. That is why Thoreau described his magic journey in Nature as a Socratic quest of "knowing thyself". Thoreau writes in chapter 18 of *Walden*:

> It is not worth the while to go round the world to count the cats in Zanzibar. Yet do this even till you can do better, and you may perhaps find some "Symmes' Hole" by which to get at the inside at last. England and France, Spain and Portugal, Gold Coast and Slave Coast, all front on this private sea; but no bark from them has ventured out of sight of land, though it is without doubt the direct way to India. If you would learn to speak all tongues and conform to the customs of all nations, if you would travel farther than all travellers, be naturalized in all climes, and cause the Sphinx to dash her head against a stone, even obey the precept of the old philosopher, and Explore thyself.[2]

Therefore, Thoreau entered a kind of philosophical fellowship with Socrates in seeking wisdom and acting virtuously from principle. For example, the eco-criticism and individualism developed in *Walden* are the two most complete Socratic statements of Thoreau's revolt against the spirit of conquest of his time. It is also worth reminding that the two main roots of Thoreau's thinking, namely environmentalism and transcendentalism, go back to his introduction to Hinduism and Buddhism through Ralph Waldo Emerson. Consequently, Thoreau's access to Ralph Waldo Emerson's library introduced him to great works of Indian philosophy such as the *Vedas*, the *Laws of Manu*, the *Bhagavad-Gita*, and *The Upanishads*.

> The divinity Thoreau found in *The Upanishads* spoke to his sense of a divine presence that is near, vital, and alive. This divinity was not remote from nature, but rather, apparent and accessible through everything—through everything but not, ultimately the thing itself.

1 Thoreau, Henry David, *Walden*, Boston: Beacon Press, 1997, 2004, p. 203.
2 Ibid., p. 301.

> The "pantheistic tone" commented upon by White that is prevalent in Walden's descriptions of nature derived from a view of divinity described in *The Upanishads* as both transcendent, overall, but also immanent. All things, all forms, rise out of the pervasive and creative forces that animate existence. In this system, one must be able to hold the paradox between the two attitudes, transcendent and immanent, in order to express a truth and experience that which cannot be communicated by either concept alone [...]. The immanent divinity celebrated in *Walden* is that each discrete thing is an expression of the universal creative force that pervades all, each part of nature is infused, overflowing, with the creative energy that gives rise to it.[3]

Thoreau followed the pantheistic rhythm of the Indian sacred literature in his *Walden*. For him, God was not only immanent in the world, but also omnipresent in Nature. As such, we can find many examples of the sacredness of Nature in *Walden*. "Thus it appears", Thoreau wrote in *Walden*,

> that the sweltering inhabitants of Charleston and New Orleans, of Madras and Bombay and Calcutta, drink at my well. In the morning I bathe my intellect in the stupendous and cosmogonal philosophy of the Bhagvat-Geeta, since whose composition years of the gods have elapsed, and in comparison, with which our modern world and its literature seem puny and trivial; and I doubt if that philosophy is not to be referred to a previous state of existence, so remote is its sublimity from our conceptions. I lay down the book and go to my well for water, and lo! there I meet the servant of the Bramin, priest of Brahma and Vishnu and Indra, who still sits in his temple on the Ganges reading the Vedas, or dwells at the root of a tree with his crust and water jug. I meet his servant come to draw water for his master, and our buckets as it were grate together in the same well. The pure Walden water is mingled with the sacred water of the Ganges. With favoring winds, it is wafted past the site of the fabulous islands of Atlantis and the Hesperides, makes the periplus of Hanno, and, floating by Ternate and Tidore and the mouth of the Persian Gulf, melts in the tropic gales of the Indian seas, and is landed in ports of which Alexander only heard the names.[4]

3 Cowan, Eric, Echterling, Lennis G., "Nature's Sage: The Influence of Sacred Indian Literature in Henry David Thoreau's *Walden*," *Journal of East-West Thought*, 2016, 6(4), p. 62.

4 Thoreau, Henry David, *Walden*, Boston: Beacon Press, 1997, 2004, pp. 278–279.

Living intimately with Nature was a lesson that Thoreau learnt from *The Upanishads*. As such, "part of the uniqueness of *Walden* is Thoreau's deft synthesis of the soaring universal themes of Indian sacred literature with his particular and intimate impressions of nature on the banks of Walden Pond [...] He affirmed through his loving participation with the natural world that the God that one seeks dwells within all that surrounds one. In *Walden*, there is no dualistic split between matter and spirit. One must be open to the flow between the inner world of thoughts, feelings and sensations and the perpetual instilling in which they take their form in immediate and mutual participation".[5] In other words, to Thoreau, Nature represented much more than physical materialism. Nature was a source of spiritual forces and moral values. That is why Thoreau, like Emerson, considered Nature as a critical component in the moral evolution of humanity. For Thoreau, Nature was an open door to the sanity of humankind. He wrote the following in his essay, "Life Without Principle", published posthumously in the *Atlantic Monthly* in 1863: "Really to see the sun rise or go down every day, so to relate ourselves to a universal fact, would preserve us sane forever."[6] More than being a simple act of dwelling, Thoreau considered living *in* and *with* Nature as a spiritual experience and an act of love. He asserted:

> I wish to suggest that a man may be very industrious, and yet not spend his time well. There is no more fatal blunderer than he who consumes the greater part of his life getting his living. All great enterprises are self-supporting. The poet, for instance, must sustain his body by his poetry, as a steam planing-mill feeds its boilers with the shavings it makes. You must get your living by loving. But as it is said of the merchants that ninety-seven in a hundred fail, so the life of men generally, tried by this standard, is a failure, and bankruptcy may be surely prophesied.[7]

Putting life and love together was a way for Thoreau to say that life was neither measured by material possessions and economic prosperity, nor by power and success. Unlike the focus of modern society, which was to acquire wealth and material goods, Thoreau suggested a simple life in harmony with Nature. But he took this idea further and affirmed that an affluent society

---

5 Cowan, Eric, Echterling, Lennis G., "Nature's Sage: The Influence of Sacred Indian Literature in Henry David Thoreau's *Walden,*" *Journal of East-West Thought*, 2016, 6(4), 2016, pp. 58–59.

6 Thoreau, Henry David, "Life Without Principle," in *Walden and Other Writings*, New York: The Modern Library, 2000, p. 762.

7 Ibid., p. 752.

was a barrier to the discovery of Nature's spiritual values. He made this point clear in *Walden* by going back to great philosophers of the past. He argued:

> Most of the luxuries, and many of the so-called comforts of life, are not only not indispensable, but positive hindrances to the elevation of mankind. With respect to luxuries and comforts, the wisest have ever lived a more simple and meagre life than the poor. The ancient philosophers, Chinese, Hindoo, Persian, and Greek, were a class than which none has been poorer in outward riches, none so rich in inward. We know not much about them. It is remarkable that we know so much of them as we do. The same is true of the more modern reformers and benefactors of their race. None can be an impartial or wise observer of human life but from the vantage ground of what we should call voluntary poverty. Of a life of luxury the fruit is luxury, whether in agriculture, or commerce, or literature, or art. There are nowadays professors of philosophy, but not philosophers. Yet it is admirable to profess because it was once admirable to live. To be a philosopher is not merely to have subtle thoughts, nor even to found a school, but so to love wisdom as to live according to its dictates, a life of simplicity, independence, magnanimity, and trust. It is to solve some of the problems of life, not only theoretically, but practically. The success of great scholars and thinkers is commonly a courtier-like success, not kingly, not manly. They make shift to live merely by conformity, practically as their fathers did, and are in no sense the progenitors of a noble race of men. But why do men degenerate ever? What makes families run out? What is the nature of the luxury which enervates and destroys nations? Are we sure that there is none of it in our own lives? The philosopher is in advance of his age even in the outward form of his life. He is not fed, sheltered, clothed, warmed, like his contemporaries. How can a man be a philosopher and not maintain his vital heat by better methods than other men?[8]

When we read *Walden*, we get the feeling that Thoreau's daily encounter with the surrounding Nature turns out to be a meticulous work of an ecological detective who at every step investigates and evaluates the mysteries of life. As Thoreau observed: "The universe is wider than our views of it [...]. Every man is the lord of a realm beside which the earthly empire of the Czar is but a petty state, a hummock left by the ice. Yet some can be patriotic who have no self-respect, and sacrifice the greater to the less. They love the soil which makes their graves, but have no sympathy with the spirit which may

8 Thoreau, Henry David, *Walden*, Boston: Beacon Press, 1997, 2004, pp. 12–13.

still animate their clay. Patriotism is a maggot in their heads."[9] In Thoreau's work, the reader is exposed to a new type of reading of Nature. Thoreau is one who sees the physical geography and the transcendental metaphysics of Nature. Like a private eye, Thoreau reveals to his readers different layers of the living system of Nature. Thoreau's take on the mystery of life elevates the profundity of Nature to new heights. For example, Thoreau writes in Chapter 17 of *Walden*:

> I love to see that Nature is so rife with life that myriads can be afforded to be sacrificed and suffered to prey on one another; that tender organizations can be so serenely squashed out of existence like pulp—tadpoles which herons gobble up, and tortoises and toads run over in the road; and that sometimes it has rained flesh and blood! With the liability to accident, we must see how little account is to be made of it. The impression made on a wise man is that of universal innocence. Poison is not poisonous after all, nor are any wounds fatal.[10]

No doubt, as an American transcendentalist, Thoreau's image of happiness in Nature is indissolubly bound up with the image of redemption. Rather than having a fatalist attitude, Thoreau's images of Nature are filled with spiritual reverence. Nature becomes the monumental spiritual force that propels the human pilgrim into a new understanding of life, the world, and history. On the one hand, there is an omnipresent awareness of the catastrophes of the industrial age. On the other hand, Thoreau transforms the act of looking at Nature into an art of understanding it. Thoreau wrote famously in *Walden*:

> I went to the woods because I wished to live deliberately, to front only the essential facts of life, and see if I could not learn what it had to teach, and not, when I came to die, discover that I had not lived. I did not wish to live what was not life, living is so dear; nor did I wish to practice resignation, unless it was quite necessary. I wanted to live deep and suck out all the marrow of life, to live so sturdily and Spartan-like as to put to rout all that was not life, to cut a broad swath and shave close, to drive life into a corner, and reduce it to its lowest terms, and, if it proved to be mean, why then to get the whole and genuine meanness of it, and publish its meanness to the world; or if it were sublime, to know it by experience, and be able to give a true account of it in my next excursion.[11]

---

9 Ibid., pp. 299–300.

10 Ibid., p. 297.

11 Ibid., pp. 85–86.

Thoreau most consciously and deliberately tried to understand what it might be like to be a creature of Nature. Since Thoreau believed that Nature is a reflection of God, he recognised every element of Nature as serving a unique cosmic purpose. Thoreau knew this perfectly, and that is why he stated in his conclusion of *Walden*: "The universe is wider than our views of it."[12] But, for him, the only way to comprehend this "wideness" of the universe was to choose a philosophical quest in life. For Thoreau, to understand the absolute value of life was inconceivable without living it philosophically. "To be a philosopher", argued Thoreau, "is not merely to have subtle thoughts, nor even to found a school, but so to love wisdom as to live according to its dictates, a life of simplicity, independence, magnanimity, and trust. It is to solve some of the problems of life, not only theoretically, but practically".[13]

Thoreau's aim in life was to become a morally autonomous and independent-minded person. "If our whole [life] is startlingly moral",[14] as Thoreau declared, then we can learn lessons of morality from Nature. An apostle of individual freedom, Henry David Thoreau believed that we each must find our own path to moral freedom. Certainly, Thoreau broke free from his community's influence and chose to have a solitary life in Nature, but he also demonstrated his commitment to the otherness of others by fighting slavery and refusing to participate as a citizen in the American efforts of war against Mexico. Even in criticising the society of his time and turning towards Nature, Thoreau was careful to share his way with others. He asserted:

> I learned this, at least, by my experiment: that if one advances confidently in the direction of his dreams, and endeavors to live the life which he has imagined, he will meet with a success unexpected in common hours. He will put some things behind, will pass an invisible boundary; new, universal, and more liberal laws will begin to establish themselves around and within him; or the old laws be expanded, and interpreted in his favor in a more liberal sense, and he will live with the license of a higher order of beings. In proportion as he simplifies his life, the laws of the universe will appear less complex, and solitude will not be solitude, nor poverty poverty, nor weakness weakness. If you have built castles in the air, your work need not be lost; that is where they should be. Now put the foundations under them.[15]

12 Ibid., p. 299.
13 Ibid., p. 13.
14 Ibid., p. 205.
15 Ibid., p. 303.

Thoreau serves as our Socratic guide to the self-examination of life. He also keeps us from trying to patronise Nature. His invitation to live deliberately requires an attitude of epistemic humility toward Nature. On his account, what we most need is to abandon our spirit of conquest. If such is the case, then it is no wonder that Thoreau's detractors often see him as an anarchist. Thoreau is not necessarily an anarchist in the sense of a Bakunin, but he certainly is a dissident gadfly who thinks and acts against the tide. Thoreau wrote a great deal about the meaningless culture and society which surrounded him. For example, he pointed out in *Walden* that "the mass of mean lead lives of quite desperation".[16] This discussion is presented as biting comments a few paragraphs later in the book: "The greater part of what my neighbors call good I believe in my soul to be bad, and if I repent of anything, it is very likely to be my good behavior. What demon possessed me that I behaved so well? You may say the wisest thing you can, old man—you who have lived seventy years, not without honor of a kind—I hear an irresistible voice which invites me away from all that. One generation abandons the enterprises of another like stranded vessels."[17] Thoreau's seclusion concerned more the company of human beings than that of animals and plants. What Thoreau's writings on Nature suggest is his empathetic attachment, not to call it a joyful companionship, for the living creatures. In *A Week on the Concord and Merrimack Rivers*, there is an interesting description of the wild ducks by Thoreau, which is a true expression of his investigator's eye: "I never voyaged so far in all my life. You shall see men you never heard of before, whose names you don't know, going away down through the meadows with long ducking-guns, with water-tight boots wading through the fowl-meadow grass, on bleak, wintry, distant shores, with guns at half-cock, and they shall see teal, blue-winged, green-winged, shelldrakes, whistlers, black ducks, ospreys, and many other wild and noble sights before night, such as they who sit in parlors never dream of".[18] Thoreau's kaleidoscopic view of Nature appears in every instance of his encounter with a world that he portrays as a meaningful and pluralistic ensemble. As a matter of fact, when we read Thoreau's pleas for Nature, we have the feeling that in an extraordinary manner the representations of the spectacle of Nature are in harmony with Thoreau's testimony of his senses. As such, Thoreau is a painter of the reality of the world who gives the highest idea of Nature. For Thoreau, the beauty of Nature and the silence of the stars

---

16 Ibid., p. 6.

17 Ibid., p. 9.

18 Thoreau, Henry David, "A Week on the Concord and Merrimack Rivers," in *Walden and Other Writings*, New York: The Modern Library, 2000, p. 317.

belong to the realm of the aesthetics of silence. The final passages of *A Week on the Concord and the Merrimack Rivers* clearly express this truth: "As we looked up in silence to those distant lights, we were reminded that it was a rare imagination which first taught that the stars are worlds, and had conferred a great benefit on mankind. It is recorded in the Chronicle of Bernaldez, that in Columbus's first voyage the natives "pointed towards the heavens, making signs that they believed that there was all power and holiness". We have reason to be grateful for celestial phenomena, for they chiefly answer to the ideal in man. The stars are distant and unobtrusive, but bright and enduring as our fairest and most memorable experiences. "Let the immortal depth of your soul lead you, but earnestly extend your eyes upwards."[19]

What is original about Thoreau is not only his art of contemplating Nature, but the fact that under his writing, Nature becomes something that can be photographed. Thoreau urges us to look carefully at the organisms and particles of Nature that are accessible to us, so as not to forget them. Strangely, Thoreau's eye is not intrusive; he looks at the natural landscapes and animals with awe rather than with indifference or contempt. It is obvious that for Thoreau, the fact of not knowing how to encounter Nature comes from the baseness of human beings. He observed in *Slavery in Massachusetts*: "I walk toward one of our ponds, but what signifies the beauty of nature when men are base? We walk to lakes to see our serenity reflected in them: when we are not serene, we go not to them. Who can be serene in a country where both the rulers and the ruled are without principle? The remembrance of my country spoils my walk. My thoughts are murder to the State, and involuntarily go plotting against her."[20] According to Alda Balthrop-Lewis, there is a close relationship between love of Nature and love of justice in Thoreau's writings. "For Thoreau", wrote Balthrop-Lewis,

> the woods were not only a place of peace. They were also where people of color and poor people we now consider white (largely Irish) lived and worked. In going to the woods, he opened himself to encounter with people outside his social, racial, and class position. During his time in Walden Woods, Thoreau made his world a little less segregated. He went to live in a neighborhood that had, in the generation before, been the home of formerly enslaved people and others outside of more elite Concord society. It was then the working place of Irish laborers. He traveled with and befriended an Indigenous guide. He got to know the

19 Ibid., p. 453.

20 Thoreau, Henry David, "Slavery in Massachusetts," in *Walden and Other Writings*, New York: The Modern Library, 2000, pp. 712–713.

> poor white people who also lived in the woods. In everyday ways, he tried to get to know what life was like for others.[21]

Thoreau had the keenest awareness of the correlation between the symmetry of the individual with Nature and the fraternity between human beings. He had a strong sense of responsibility to Nature and humans, but at the same time, he felt heavily concerned with the task of serving others. Yet, it is well-known that Thoreau decried complacency and conformity and invited his fellow Americans to be independent-minded. "Accordingly, Thoreau suggests that to genuinely help other people, one must free them from the community so that they each can follow their own paths. Philanthropy, for example, often does more harm than good because it stems from the view that people are urgently needy when they lack what the community esteems, so philanthropy tends to convey or reinforce the assumption that what the community esteems most highly really is most important."[22]

To Thoreau, philanthropy was not fraternity, since he believed the latter is a realm of superimposed feelings. In the manner of Saint Francis of Assisi, Thoreau felt a fraternal closeness and proximity with the animal world. Saint Francis was considered the man of the gospel of fraternity. He added an ecological perspective to the non-violent message of Jesus Christ. Francis and his brothers claimed a new evangelical way of life, marked by non-violence, fraternity, and compassion for all living beings. This compassionate and non-violent attitude of Saint Francis in relation to all elements of life can be found in his famous prayer: "Lord, make me an instrument of your peace. Where there is hatred, let me sow love; where there is injury, pardon; where there is doubt, faith; where there is despair, hope; where there is darkness, light; and where there is sadness, joy."[23] Though Thoreau was not a Franciscan, there are strong moments of fraternalization with Nature, which bring reminders of Saint Francis's hymns of praise for the stars and the birds. In Chapter 9 of *Walden*, Thoreau praises the Pond for its purity and transparency. Thoreau observed:

> Walden is a perfect forest mirror, set round with stones as precious to my eye as if fewer or rarer. Nothing so fair, so pure, and at the same time so

---

21 Balthrop-Lewis, *Thoreau's Religion: Walden Woods, Social Justice, and the Politics* of *Asceticism*, Cambridge: Cambridge University Press, 2021, pp. 10–11.

22 Mason, Marshall, "Freedom through Critique: Thoreau's Service to Others," *Transactions of the Charles S. Peirce Society*, 2005, 41(2), p. 403.

23 Quoted in Ramakrishnan, Ram, *Many Paths, One Destination: Love, Peace, Compassion*, Wheatmark: Arizona, 2009, p. 32.

> large, as a lake, perchance, lies on the surface of the earth. Sky water. It needs no fence. Nations come and go without defiling it. It is a mirror which no stone can crack, whose quicksilver will never wear off, whose gilding Nature continually repairs; no storms, no dust, can dim its surface ever fresh;—a mirror in which all impurity presented to it sinks, swept and dusted by the sun's hazy brush,—this the light dust-cloth,—which retains no breath that is breathed on it, but sends its own to float as clouds high above its surface, and be reflected in its bosom still.[24]

Thoreau's trip to Walden Pond was a journey of self-discovery. That is why Nature was represented by Thoreau as a magical entity that enabled his mystical fellowship with God and the world. As such, under Thoreau's pen, Nature (and not Man) became the measure of all things. For him, Nature was the meeting point between the ontological and the experiential. Accordingly, Thoreau insisted on experiencing the full sensory impact of Nature, in which the self and the world are no more than one element. We can find traces of this mode of thinking in Thoreau's *Journal*. The following passage is dated March 12, 1853:

> It is essential that a man confine himself to pursuits—a scholar, for instance, to studies—which lie next to and conduce to his life, which do not go against the grain, either of his will or his imagination. The scholar finds in his experience some studies to be moist, fertile and radiant with light, others dry, barren, and dark. If he is wise, he will not persevere in the last, as a plant in a cellar will strive toward the light. He will confine the observations of his mind as closely as possible to the experience or life of his senses. His thought must live with and be inspired with the life of the body. The death-bed scenes and observations even of the best and wisest afford but a sorry picture of our humanity. Some men endeavor to live a constrained life, to subject their whole lives to their will, as he who said he would give a sign if he were conscious after his head was cut off,—but he gave no sign. Dwell as near as possible to the channel in which your life flows. A man may associate with such companions, he may pursue such employments, as will darken the day for him. Men choose darkness rather than light.[25]

---

24 Thoreau, Henry David, *Walden*, Boston: Beacon Press, 1997, 2004, p. 178.

25 Thoreau, Henry David, *I to Myself: An Annotated Selection from the Journal of Henry D. Thoreau*, edited by Jeffrey S. Cramer, New Haven: Yale University Press, 2008, pp. 181–182.

Henry David Thoreau was a multi-visionary who stood between the East and the West. Thereby, he swam in Walden Pond as if he was taking a spiritual bath in the sacred water of the Ganges. Nature, for Thoreau, was the open book of life, a geography without borders. That being the case, Thoreau remains a key figure in the process of self-maturation of humanity in its efforts to rediscover its ecological imperatives. The Waldenian lessons of Thoreau are ours today, not just because he lived in simple near isolation at Walden Pond, but because in his essay "Walking" he wrote: "I wish to speak a word for Nature, for absolute freedom and wildness, as contrasted with a freedom and culture merely civil,—to regard man as an inhabitant, or a part and parcel of Nature, rather than a member of society. I wish to make an extreme statement, if so I may make an emphatic one, for there are enough champions of civilization: the minister and the school committee and every one of you will take care of that."[26]

26 Thoreau, Henry David, "Walking," in *Walden and Other Writings*, New York: The Modern Library, 2000, p. 627.

Chapter 2

MAHATMA GANDHI: NON-VIOLENCE AND NATURE

Although he did not write directly on environmental issues, Mahatma Gandhi can be considered one of the precursors of the environmentalist movement in India and around the globe. His ideas on Swaraj, village industry, self-sufficiency, appropriate technologies, and decentralised democracy had a great impact on key figures like Ernst Friedrich Schumacher and Vandana Shiva in the past 70 years. Gandhi was very attentive and far-sighted in relation to the problems of Nature. He believed that the universe was created by a cosmic spirit which made all creation equal. He observed: "I believe in the essential unity of man and for that matter of all that lives. Therefore, I believe that if one man gains spiritually, the whole world gains with him and, if one man falls, the whole world falls to that extent."[1] Gandhi also believed in the harmony and cooperation between humans and other living beings. In other words, he judged the world of humans in the mirror of the animal world. He famously said: "The greatness of a nation and its moral progress can be judged by the way its animals are treated."[2]

With this ecological perspective as the foundation of his intellectual background, it is no surprise that the Gandhian philosophy of life and action has tried at every historical instance to protect the environment and promote living democracy simultaneously. Gandhi saw humankind as part of Nature rather than cut off from Nature. According to him, such a perspective of human ecology would help humankind to become truly humane. Here, then, was a moral leader and a man in search of truth, who was in harmony and peace with Nature. He was a practitioner of ecological sustainability in

1 Gandhi, Mohandas Karamchand, *All Men Are Brothers*, compiled and edited by Krishna Kripalani, Ahmedabad: Navajivan Publishing House, 1971, p. 188.

2 Gandhi, Mahatma, *Quotes of Mahatma Gandhi*, edited by D. Brewer, Wisdom Collection Book, published by Lulu.com, 2020, p. 81.

the real sense of the word, combining environmental necessities and ethical priorities. According to Gandhian scholar N. Radhakrishnan,

> The ashrams or the communities Gandhi founded, both in South Africa and in India, were meaningful centres where Gandhi demonstrated with convincing success how each member of this community could live in harmony with nature. The community life Gandhi was developing consisted of manual labour, tree planting, agriculture, simple life, and crafts. In short, they were attempts at self-sufficiency without invoking the blessings of the temptation from outside. While they could be described to be bold experiments, but by no stretch of imagination could anyone say they were utopian ideals. The running and recurrent principle of the community life was to live according to the rhythm of nature and in harmony with nature with minimum needs and not to exploit nature beyond taking what nature offers.[3]

Subsequently, the decentralised approach of Mahatma Gandhi to the World House, where humans live in peace with animals and plants, and where sustainability is a way of life, opened new perspectives in ethical responsibility towards the planet Earth. Gandhi's philosophy of life was founded on the belief in the holistic development of human beings marked by the quest of truth and non-violence. As such, Gandhi's environmental engagement became achievable with human moral capability and in harmony with the laws of Nature. Gandhi described these laws as "changeless and unchangeable [...] [with] no miracles in the sense of infringement or interruption of Nature's laws".[4] Since Gandhi followed the Advaita philosophy for his understanding of Nature and humankind's relationship to it, he established an interconnectedness between the individual and the animal kingdom. It is important to note that when Gandhi was speaking of interconnectedness and harmony between humans and animals, he was referring to an ethics of living together beyond the theory of evolution by natural selection. Gandhi wrote: "My ethics not only permit me to claim but require me to own kinship with not merely the ape, but the horse and the sheep, the lion and the leopard, the snake and the scorpion."[5] This Gandhian ontological interconnection with animals found its essence in the bare truth that life is endangered continuously by violence. According to

3 Quoted in Khoshoo, T.N., *Mahatma Gandhi: An Apostle of Applied Human Ecology*, New Delhi: Tata Energy Research Institute, 1995, p. 10.

4 Gandhi, Mohandas Karamchand, *Truth is God*, compiled by R.K. Prabhu, Ahmedabad: Navajivan Publishing House, 1955, p. 23.

5 Ibid., p. 116.

Gandhi, "All life in the flesh exists by some Himsa. Hence the highest religion has been defined by a negative word Ahimsa. The world is bound in a chain of destruction. In other words Himsa is an inherent necessity for life in the body. That is why a votary of Ahimsa always prays for ultimate deliverance from the bondage of the flesh."[6] However, Gandhi distinguished very clearly between the structural violence of human beings and the instinctive sense of self-preservation in animals. That is why he abhorred all attacks against living creatures and their natural surroundings. In this connection, he affirmed:

> I do not want to live at the cost of the life even of a snake. I should let him bite me to death rather than kill him. But it is likely that if God puts me to that cruel test and permits a snake to assault me, I may not have the courage to die, but that the beast in me may assert itself and I may seek to kill the snake in defending this perishable body. I admit that my belief has not become incarnate in me as to warrant my stating emphatically that I have shed all fear of snakes so as to befriend them as I would like to be able to. It is my implicit belief that snakes, tigers, etc. are God's answer to the poisonous, wicked, evil thoughts we harbour. [...] I believe that all life is one. Thoughts take definite forms. Tigers and snakes have kinship with us. They are a warning to us to avoid harbouring evil, wicked, lustful thoughts. If I want to rid the earth of venomous beasts and reptiles, I must rid myself of all venomous thoughts. I shall not do so if in my impatient ignorance and in my desire to prolong the existence of the body I seek to kill the so-called venomous beasts and reptiles. If in not seeking to defend myself against such noxious animals, I die, I should rise again a better and fuller man. With that faith in me how should I seek to kill a fellow being in a snake?[7]

Gandhi's philosophy of Nature points to an indivisible whole that cannot be segregated into disconnected compartments. In fact, as we saw above, Gandhi's concept of Nature is a universal, inclusive, and self-enacting one. As such, the very first responsibility of human beings is service to the Universe, because from Gandhi's point of view such an ecological imperative would stand for the spiritual emancipation of the human soul in the *dharmic* phase of environmentalism. Gandhi did not refer to dharma as a religious concept, but he understood it as an ethical concept and a moral code. Accordingly, Gandhi's view of the relationship between humankind and Nature was based on the Vedic perception of Earth as the Universal Mother (*Dharti Mata*).

---

6 Ibid., p. 118.

7 Ibid., pp. 117–118.

Furthermore, Gandhi looked upon Earth as an emerging and maturing phenomenon that preserves life. In this context, Gandhi saw humankind as the only animal who knows its Maker and has a duty to help and serve its fellow beings. He stated: "It is an arrogant assumption to say that human beings are lords and masters of the lower creatures. On the contrary, being endowed with greater things in life, they are the trustees of the lower animal kingdom."[8] For Gandhi, one of the most dangerous characteristics of human rationality was its epistemological arrogance which revealed itself in the modern Cartesian goal of mastery of Nature. According to Descartes, by "knowing the force and actions of the fire, water, air and stars, the heavens, and all other bodies that surround us, just as we understand the various skills of our craftsmen, we could make ourselves the masters and possessors of nature."[9] Gandhi, however, argued the exact opposite of Descartes by saying that, "it is an arrogant assumption to say that human beings are lords and masters of the lower creatures. On the contrary, being endowed with greater things in life, they are the trustees of the lower animal kingdom."[10]

Being ontologically and epistemologically conscious of the place and role of humankind in the Universe, Gandhi gave human beings the role of trustees of all other living creatures and actors of the welfare of others. More importantly, Gandhi used the concept of *Yajna* to describe the indebtedness of humans to Nature. He asserted: "*Yajna* means an act directed to the welfare of others, done without desiring any return for it, whether of a temporal or spiritual nature. 'Act' here must be taken in its widest sense, and includes thoughts and word, as well as deed. 'Others' embraces not only humanity, but all life. Therefore, and from the standpoint of ahimsa, it is not a *Yajna* to sacrifice lower animals even with a view to the service of humanity."[11] As a result, we can say that for Gandhi, *Yajna* is an act of empathy and compassion accompanied by a dimension of epistemic humility. Humility is also the thread running throughout Gandhi's ethical approach to Nature. Gandhi indeed helped us find an answer to the difficult challenge of combining natural togetherness

8 Quoted in Khoshoo, T.N., *Mahatma Gandhi: An Apostle of Applied Human Ecology*, New Delhi: Tata Energy Research Institute, 1995, p. 18.

9 Descartes, René, *Discourse on the Method*, translated by Donald A. Cress, Indianapolis: Hackett, 1985. See Richard Kennington, "Rene Descartes," in *History of Political Philosophy*, edited by Leo Strauss and Joseph Cropsey, 3rd ed., Chicago: University of Chicago Press, 1987, pp. 421–439.

10 Quoted in Khoshoo, T.N., *Mahatma Gandhi: An Apostle of Applied Human Ecology*, New Delhi: Tata Energy Research Institute, 1995, p. 18.

11 Gandhi, Mohandas Karamchand, *Truth is God*, compiled by R.K. Prabhu, Ahmedabad: Navajivan Publishing House, 1955, p. 139.

with biodiversity. Gandhi's acceptance of biological differences in the world and the recognition of shared life values between humankind and other living beings were paths for him to challenge the reductionist nature of the modern techno-scientific system. Gandhi knew well that humanity needs an ecological mind to address ecological issues. As such, for Gandhi, the conservation of biodiversity was a question of ethics and living plurality. That is why, in this process of Earth democracy, he included all living creatures and recognised three imperatives of interconnected life on Earth: first, every living being is part of the Earth's extended family; second, every living being has the right to life; and third, life on Earth should be accompanied by a sustainable decentralised living democracy.

Thinking about the unity of all life on the planet Earth, Gandhi stated the following in his famous speech at Kingsley Hall in 1931: "There is an orderliness in the universe, there is an unalterable law governing everything and every being that exists or lives. It is no blind law; for no blind law can govern the conduct of living beings."[12] Obviously, looking at the development process in India in the 1930–1940s, Mahatma Gandhi was more inclined to think and to realise the ecological imperatives of the time through local self-sufficiency and empowerment of villages. Therefore, based on his experience of the ground realities and the exploitation of villages by the big cities, he came to this conclusion:

> I regard the growth of cities as an evil thing, unfortunate for mankind and the world, unfortunate for England and certainly unfortunate for India. The British have exploited India through its cities. The latter have exploited the villages. The blood of the villages is the cement with which the edifice of the cities is built. I want the blood that is today inflating the arteries of the cities to run once again in the blood vessels of the villagers [...]. We are inheritors of a rural civilization. The vastness of our country, the vastness of the population, the situation and the climate of the country have, in my opinion, destined it for a rural civilization. Its defects are well known but not one of them is irremediable. To uproot it and substitute for it an urban civilization seems to me an impossibility, unless we are prepared by some drastic means to reduce the population from three hundred million to three or say even thirty. I can therefore suggest remedies on the assumption that we must

---

12 Quoted in Khoshoo, T.N., *Mahatma Gandhi: An Apostle of Applied Human Ecology*, New Delhi: Tata Energy Research Institute, 1995, p. 30.

> perpetuate the present rural civilization and endeavour to rid it of its acknowledged defects.[13]

Gandhi's philosophy of the welfare of the weakest (*Antodaya*) leading to the welfare of all (*Sarvodaya*) included not only the poor but also the weakest living beings. Gandhi's ideal village was not free of animals and plants, since "every man [had] an equal right to the necessaries of life even as birds and beasts [had]."[14] His sustainable life-saving approach was a *Swaraj*-based bottom-up shared view, rather than a corporate top-down authoritarian and centralised outlook. Therefore, Gandhi's ecological mode of thinking provided a picture of mutual dependence among humans and with other living beings inhabiting the world. Accordingly, Gandhi added that such a society "must naturally be based on truth and non-violence which [...] are not possible without a living belief in God, meaning a Self-existent, All-knowing Living Force which [inhered] every other force known to the world."[15] Needless to say, among the ecological imperatives put forward by Gandhi, sanitation in the villages played an important role in the relationship between humankind and Nature. For Gandhi, a healthy village was only possible with villagers possessing a healthy mind and a healthy body. Gandhi categorically underlined: "Anyone who fouls the air by spitting about carelessly, throwing refuse and rubbish, or otherwise dirtying the ground, sins against man and Nature [...] We do not mind dirtying the well or the tank or the river by whose side or in which we perform ablution. I regard this defect as a great vice which is responsible for the disgraceful state of our villages and the sacred banks of the sacred rivers and for the diseases that spring that spring from insanitation."[16]

Gandhi's environmental approach to life and society was symbolised by his concept of the oceanic circle in opposition to the corporate and technocratic pyramidal structure of society and state. As Gandhi described it:

> In this structure composed of innumerable villages, there will be ever widening, never ascending circles. Life will not be a pyramid with the apex sustained by the bottom. But it will be an oceanic circle whose center will be the individual always ready to perish for the village, the latter ready to perish for the circle of villages, till at last the whole

13 Gandhi, Mohandas Karamchand, *Village Swaraj*, Ahmedabad: Navajivan Publishing, 1962, pp. 22, 26, 27.

14 Ibid., p. 33.

15 Ibid., p. 67.

16 Quoted in Khoshoo, T.N., *Mahatma Gandhi: An Apostle of Applied Human Ecology*, New Delhi: Tata Energy Research Institute, 1995, p. 66.

> becomes one life composed of individuals, never aggressive in their arrogance but ever humble, sharing the majesty of the oceanic circle of which they are integral units. Therefore, the outermost circumference will not wield power to crust the inner circle but will give strength to all within and derive its own strength from it. I may be taunted with the retort that this is all Utopian and, therefore, not worth a single thought. If Euclid's point, though incapable of being drawn by human agency, has an imperishable value, my picture has its own for mankind to live. Let India live for this true picture, though never realizable in its completeness. We must have a proper picture of what we want before we can have something approaching it. If there ever is to be a republic of every village in India then I claim verity for my picture in which the last is equal to the first or, in other words, no one is to be the first and none the last.[17]

Gandhi applied the spirit of economic and political decentralisation and service and love in the context of the exchange of necessities of life. He further outlined his vision of the relationship between humankind and Nature by making a departure from the modern conception of bureaucracy and hierarchy. As Praveen Dhanda explains clearly:

> A reformed individual is as important aspect of Gandhi's thought bearing implications on his concepts like oceanic circle. It necessitates moral issues like ethics of consumption and "bread labour" which are important part of Gandhi's worldview with reference to creation of such an individual. Gandhi insists on "bread labour" by everyone and persistently emphasised the importance of work in human being's personal growth. The essence here is to emphasise the dignity of physical and manual labour. Bread labour involves that people gain satisfaction, utilities, and enjoyment from work. Any technology which dehumanises people is not consistent with bread labour, however there will be a good amount of far more modern technology, of a different kind, which complement the idea of bread labour. Thus, the work according to the idea of bread labour is a creative work and, in Gandhi's framework, only possible in a society in which crushing hierarchies are absent. This is in contrast with the nature of production in modern techno-industrial pyramidic systems which focus only on means to earn a livelihood, on a single monotonous work through the use of dehumanising technology

17 Gandhi, Mohandas Karamchand, *Panchayat Raj*, Ahmedabad: Navajivan Publishing, 1959, pp. 13–14.

> leading to alienation and "joyless economy" under the conditions of hierarchical systems. Similarly, to create an ideal "individual", Gandhi argues against unbridled consumption and multiplication of desires. This idea asserts that an "individual's welfare is best achieved not, as economic theory suggests, by attempting to maximise the satisfaction of a multiplicity of desires subject only to the prevailing budget constraint, but rather by reflecting on one's desires and trying to choose between them". His insights on ethics of consumption are central to the individual's conception of self her/his relationship with the society and the nature. Gandhi also advocated a multifaceted constructive programme to rejuvenate the individual and society at large.[18]

To follow the anti-corporate mindset of Gandhi's idea of the individual and its opposition to the hierarchical and centralised organisation of Nature, we can also evaluate his concept of self-reliance through the lens of his moral philosophy, which is practised against the modern paradigm of sovereignty. Undoubtedly, either in the domain of politics or that of human relations with Nature, Gandhi believed in the idea of shared sovereignty as a regulatory principle of human community and humankind's relation with the living world. Interestingly, Gandhi believed that not only shared sovereignty could improve harmony between communities, but also with animals, since humans too often claimed power in exclusive terms. As a matter of fact, Gandhi had the courage to stand up and talk back to the authority of tradition and the epistemological arrogance of modernity. Gandhi was very conscious of the fact that an inclusive vision of reality and the cultivation of a living pluralism extended to plants and animals required a new consciousness that objected to all forms of paternalism. Moreover, according to Gandhi, this new ecological sensibility provided the moral foundation for the reintegration of "wilderness" in the work of civilisation and as an everyday experience for human beings. Finally, Gandhi also knew that adopting an ecological perspective might have certain democratic implications conducive to engendering the potential for self-realization (*Swaraj*) and sustainable life (*Swadeshi*). As Gandhi argued: "If Swaraj was not meant to civilize us, and to purify and stabilize our civilization, it would be nothing worth. The very essence of our civilization is that we give a paramount place to morality in all our affairs, public or private [...]. The very connotation of the word and the means of its attainment to which we are pledged—truth and non-violence-precludes all possibility of

18 Dhanda, Praveen, "Beyond the Pyramidic Structures: Gandhi's Vision of Oceanic Circle," *Nainital: Journal of Acharya Narendra Dev Research Institute*, Jan 2019–Jun 2019, 27, p. 58.

that Swaraj being more for some one than for the other, being partial to some and prejudicial to others."[19] In other words, in the eyes of Mahatma Gandhi, Swaraj was considered a service to the whole world. He believed in Swaraj not only as a national or political entity but as a fraternal relationship with the world. He came to regard the world as a place for fraternity with no borders. Thus, Gandhi was wary about the absence of this fraternity regarding animals. He wrote: "I do feel that spiritual progress does demand at some stage that we should cease to kill our fellow creatures for the satisfaction of our bodily wants [...]. I do not regard flesh-food as necessary for us at any stage and under any clime in which it is possible for human beings ordinarily to live, I hold flesh-food to be unsuited to our species."[20]

Gandhi's use of the concept of *Swadeshi* also included the protection of animals. According to Gandhi, *Swadeshi* was achievable not only through voluntary and participatory social action but also as a form of neighborliness to all living beings. Therefore, in Gandhi's vision of *Swadeshi*, the idea of sustainability stood next to that of ecological equity. Gandhi described *Swadeshi* as "that spirit in us which restricts us to the use and service of our immediate surroundings to the exclusion of the more remote. It is easy to undo the evil if the thinking portion of the community were to take the Swadeshi vow, even though it may for a time cause considerable inconvenience. I hate legislative interference in any department of life."[21] Maybe, that is why Gandhi described *Swadeshi* as "law of laws"[22] inscribed in the essence of human beings. For him, *Swadeshi* as a fraternal duty towards the immediate neighbour was a love of the world (Amor Mundi) which was translated by serving the living beings. As such, Gandhi believed that the implementation of *Swadeshi* in the environmental domain called for the protection of all the animals and plants, starting with the cow, which was considered a sacred animal by the Hindu faith. Gandhi wrote:

> Cow protection to me is one of the most wonderful phenomena in human evolution. It takes the human being beyond this species. The cow to me means the entire sub-human world. Man through the cow is enjoined to realize his identity with all that lives. Why the cow was

19 Gandhi, Mohandas Karamchand, *Village Swaraj*, Ahmedabad: Navajivan Publishing, 1962, p. 3.

20 Gandhi, Mohandas Karamchand, *India of My Dreams*, Ahmedabad: Navajivan Publishing, 1947, pp. 162–163.

21 Ibid., pp. 123, 127.

22 Gandhi, Mohandas Karamchand, *From Yervada Mandir*, Ahmedabad: Navajivan, 2007, p. 35.

> selected for apotheosis is obvious to me. The cow was in India the best companion. She was the giver of plenty. Not only did she give milk, but she also made agriculture possible. The cow is a poem of pity. One reads pity in the gentle animal. She is the mother to millions of Indian mankind. Protection of the cow means protection of the whole dumb creation of God. The ancient seer, whoever he was, began with the cow. The appeal of the lower order of creation is all the more forcible because it is speechless.[23]

Being environmentally conscious, Gandhi was well aware of the fact that vegetarianism was the best way to apply the ethics of non-violence and compassion to all animals. In fact, a close examination of Gandhian principles of non-violence reveals that all through his life Gandhi explored and practised social and political interrelationships by giving priority to ecological imperatives. The best example, which immediately comes to mind, is during his collaboration with the Khilafat movement when Gandhi urged the Ali brothers (Maulana Mohammad Ali and Maulana Shaukat Ali) to refrain from cow slaughter. Gandhi wanted to guarantee the matter of cow protection in the Indian Muslim community. That is why he "treated the Khilafat as a 'Kamadhuk', the mythical cow that gave whatever one asked of her."[24] Later Gandhi explained: "I have been telling Maulana Shaukat Ail [*sic* for Ali] all along that I was helping him to save his cow, i.e., the Khilafat, because I hoped to save my cow thereby."[25] Not surprisingly, the Ali brothers and many other leaders of the Khilafat movement promised on behalf of the Indian Muslims that when India wins independence, one of the regulations would be the prohibition of cow slaughter. Therefore, "as a gesture toward Hindus, Muhammad Ali stopped eating beef; departing from age-old practice, numerous Muslim homes celebrated Eid without beef."[26]

By rising above the modern divide between humankind and other living beings, Gandhi wanted to halt the technocratic-bureaucratic mindset which limited people's good sense as citizens of the Universe. The good of all living creatures was what Gandhi envisioned. Thus, he had risen above the

23 Gandhi, Mohandas Karamchand, *India of My Dreams*, Ahmedabad: Navajivan Publishing, 1947, p. 130.

24 Qureishi, Naeem M., *Pan-Islam in British Indian Politics: A Study of the Khilafat Movement, 1918–1924*, Leiden: Brill, 1999, p. 104.

25 *Young India*, 1924–1926, 1327, quoted by Qureishi, Naeem M., *Pan-Islam in British Indian Politics: A Study of the Khilafat Movement, 1918–1924*, Leiden: Brill, 1999, p. 104.

26 Gandhi, Rajmohan, *Mohandas: A True Story of* a *Man, His People, and* an *Empire*, New Delhi: Penguin Books, 2007, p. 252.

difference of "we humans" and "they non-humans" and the insularity it bred. Gandhi's vision was that of an ideal society organised around the spiritual oneness of all living beings with interconnection and interdependence. But we also find in Gandhi, in relation to Nature and ecological imperatives, the concept of "care" for animals. Interestingly, "care for the cow" (*gau seva*) was a way for Gandhi to end religious communalism and forge Hindu-Muslim unity. Making his stand very clear, Gandhi asserted:

> Though I regard cow-protection as the central fact of Hinduism, central because it is common to the classes as well as the masses, I have never been able to understand the antipathy towards the Musalmans on that score. We say nothing about the slaughter that daily takes place on behalf of Englishmen: Our anger becomes red hot when a Musalman slaughters a cow. All the riots that have taken place in the name of cow have been an insane waste of efforts. They have not saved a single cow, but they have, on the contrary, stiffened the backs of the Musalmans and resulted in more slaughter [...]. Cow protection should commence with ourselves. In no parts of the world perhaps are cattle worse treated than in India. I have wept to see Hindu drivers goading their jaded oxen with the iron points of their cruel stick. The half-starved condition of the majority of our cattle is a disgrace to. The cows find their necks under the butcher's knife because Hindus sell them. The only effective and honourable way is to befriend the Musalmans and leave it to their Honour to save the cow. Cow protection societies most turn their attention to the feeding of cattle, prevention of cruelty, preservation of the fast-disappearing pastureland, improving the breed of cattle, buying from poor shepherds and turning pinjrapols in to middle self-supporting dairies. Hindus do sin against God and Man when they omit to do any of the things I have described above. They commit no sin, if they cannot prevent cow slaughter at the hands of Musalmans, and they do sin grievously when in other to save the cow, they quarrel with the Musalmans."[27]

It goes without saying that Gandhi's fundamental conviction about non-violence was also because of his cosmic experiment and fellowship with Nature. Gandhi's deep friendship with animals was because of his love for all living beings. He wanted to establish a new world order that emphasized on the unity of life and was based on our needs and not on our wants. Today,

---

27 Gandhi, Mohandas Karamchand, *India of My Dreams*, Ahmedabad: Navajivan Publishing, 1947, pp. 251–252.

Gandhi's holistic perception of the environment represents a moral and pragmatic guideline in our everyday actions and decision-making towards Mother Earth. Since Mahatma Gandhi's assassination in 1948, there has been a growing number of environmental concerns, including climate change, pollution, environmental degradation, resource depletion, and so on. However, as Walter Baber and Robert Bartlett say: "modernity needs to know that environmental protection can (and must) become a norm of culture rather than a mere fact of modern government."[28] Gandhi did not have the approach of a strategist in his ecological struggle, but his ethical conduct in respect to any environmental issue and towards the respect of living beings was supported by an ecological rationality. As a matter of fact, we can say that Gandhi's moral and spiritual capacities for thinking and practising Green democracy made his philosophy of non-violence not only necessary but also possible.

28 Baber F. Walter, Bartlett, Robert V., *Deliberative Environmental Politics: Democracy and Ecological Rationality*, Cambridge: The MIT Press, 2005, p. 13.

Chapter 3

RABINDRANATH TAGORE: WHOLENESS AND UNITY

Can one speak of Rabindranath Tagore and Nature in the same breath? Certainly, if we agree that Tagore's philosophical task was to glorify the divine fabric of the world and to understand its greatness, then we can consider him a philosopher of Nature and a poet whose mind and verb were influenced by the wilderness and the surrounding living beings. There is a certain vision of harmony and unity with Nature that one can find in all of Tagore's writings. For Tagore, Nature is what gives meaning to Man's life. It is in Nature that Man has glimpses of God and the fullness of reality. As he wrote in *The Religion of Man*,

> I have expressed my belief that the first stage of my realization was through my feeling of intimacy with Nature—not that Nature which has its channel of information for our mind and physical relationship with our living body, but that which satisfies our personality with manifestations that make our life rich and stimulate our imagination in their harmony of forms, colours, sounds and movements. It is not that world which vanishes into abstract symbols behind its own testimony to Science, but that which lavishly displays its wealth of reality to our personal self having its own perpetual reaction upon our human nature.[1]

Drawing from his direct experience of Nature during his childhood in Bengal, Tagore developed a sense of harmony with his natural surroundings, which he later used in his theory of education. In his essay *Personality*, Tagore underlines the "spirit of unity" which removes the dichotomy of individual and universal will, preparing a perfect harmony between Man's nature and Nature-in-general. Therefore, according to Tagore, the process of ever-becoming humanity is constantly working with the urge of synchronising ourselves with the universe. As Tagore observed:

1 Tagore, Rabindranath, *The Religion of Man*, Boston: Beacon Press, 1966, p. 18.

> We have come to this world to accept it, not merely to know it. We may become powerful by knowledge, but we attain fullness by sympathy. The highest education is that which does not merely give us information but makes our life in harmony with all existence. But we find that this education of sympathy is not only systematically ignored in schools, but it is severely repressed. From our very childhood habits are formed and knowledge is imparted in such a manner that our life is weaned away from nature and our mind and the world are set in opposition from the beginning of our days. Thus the greatest of educations for which we came prepared is neglected, and we are made to lose our world to find a bagful of information instead. We rob the child of his earth to teach him geography, of language to teach him grammar. His hunger is for the Epic, but he is supplied with chronicles of facts and dates [...]. Child-nature protests against such calamity with all its power of suffering, subdued at last into silence by punishment.[2]

In this regard, Tagore believed in the interaction between Man and Nature, as he also exhorted humanity to find harmony and cosmic fellowship. Talking about the oneness with the universe and with God, he asserted,

> The first stage towards freedom is the Santam, the true peace, which can be attained by subduing self; the next stage is the Sivam, the true goodness, which is the activity of the soul when self is subdued; and then the Advaitam, the love, the oneness with all and with God. Of course, this division is merely logical; these stages, like rays of light, may be simultaneous or divided according to the circumstances, and their order may be altered, such as the Sivam leading to Santam. But all we must know is that the Santam, Sivam, Advaitam, is the only goal for which we live and struggle.[3]

Tagore was opposed to human arrogance regarding animals and plants, and he was a severe critic of paternalism and chauvinism fomented by nationalists. He recurrently saw an ongoing nexus between the absence of unity of the self and the absence of harmony with life. To him, humankind was multidimensional and many-sided. As a result, his vision of Nature was not a static one, and he advocated biodiversity and creative exchange among living beings. As Kathleen M. O'Connell affirms correctly: "It is likely that

---

2 Tagore, Rabindranath, *Personality*, Delhi: Macmillan India, 1980, pp. 116–117.

3 Tagore, Rabindranath, *Letters to a Friend: Rabindranath Tagore's Letters to C.F. Andrews*, New Delhi: Rupa, 2002, p. 50.

Rabindranath, were he living today, would be at the forefront of those trying to save our fragile ecosystem."[4] Likewise, many of his writings clearly reflect his intimacy with Nature. He explained Mother Earth in the following words:

> My imaginary sometimes behaved exactly in the way that human beings are behaving on this earth, fast exhausting the stores of sustenance not because they must live their normal life but because they strain their capacity to live to a pitch of monstruous excess. Mother Earth has enough for the healthy appetites of her children and something extra for rare cases of abnormality. But she has not nearly enough for the sudden growth of a whole world of spoilt and pampered children. Man has been digging holes into the very foundations, not only of his livelihood, but also of his life; he is feeding upon his own body. The reckless wastage is best seen in the villages, where the light of life is being dimmed, the joy of existence dulled, the threads of social communion snapped. It should be our mission to restore the circulation of life's blood into these maltreated limbs of society; to bring to the villages health and knowledge; wealth of space in which to live; wealth of time in which to work, rest and enjoy; respect which will give them dignity; sympathy which will make them realize their kinship with the world of men, and not merely their subservient position.[5]

In Tagore's philosophy, villages are given high priority to towns as spaces of harmony with Nature and symbols of dedication to civic welfare. Again, the fact was that Tagore refused to accept the moral perversion of the cities and their exploitation of villages. According to Tagore,

> Such a moral perversion has reached its extreme length to-day in the relationship of the city and the village. The city, which is the professional aspect of society, has gradually come to believe that the village is its legitimate field for exploitation, that the village must at the cost of its own life maintain the city in all its brilliance of luxuries and excesses; that its wealth must be magnified even though that should involve the bankruptcy of happiness. True happiness is not at all expensive, because it depends upon that natural spring of beauty and life which

4 O'Connell, Kathleen M., "Tagore and Education: Creativity, Mutuality and Survival," in *The Poet and His World: Critical Essays on Rabindranath Tagore*, edited by Mohammad A. Quayum, New Delhi: Orient BlackSwan, 2011, p. 122.

5 Tagore, Rabindranath, *The Sky of Indian History: Themes and Thoughts of Rabindranath Tagore*, Compiled and edited by S. Jeyaseela Stephen, New Delhi: UBS Publishers, 2010, pp. 238–239.

> is harmony of relationship. Ambition pursues its path of self-seeking by breaking this bond of harmony, cutting gaps, creating dissensions. It feels no hesitations in trampling underfoot the harvest field, which is for all, in order to snatch away in haste the object of its craving. Today this ambition, wasteful and therefore disruptive of social life, has usurped the helm of society.[6]

Based on this approach, Tagore was convinced that Man can comprehend the universe and not exploit Nature. In a nutshell, just like Gandhi, he suggested a holistic picture of the Eternal Man connected to the whole Universe. Tagore commented, "When our wants are moderate, the rations we each claim do not exhaust the common store of nature and the pace of their restoration does not fall hopelessly behind that of our consumption. This moderation leaves us leisure to cultivate happiness, that happiness which is the artist soul of the human world, and which can create beauty of form and rhythm of life. But man today forgets that the divinity within him is revealed by the halo of this happiness."[7] How wise and acute these words of Tagore have turned out to be after a century of human destruction of Nature. It is, thus, no surprise that Tagore is considered a realist writer when it comes to the relation between humankind and wilderness. He explained this relationship in the following terms: "At one time I used to rove down Bengal's rivers, and I observed the wonderful way of life of Bengal's villages [...]. I would say there is no lack of realism in my stories. I wrote from what I saw, what I felt in my heart—my direct experience [...]"[8] Following in the footsteps of Tagore, we can understand how he related closely the unity of life and that of humankind. For Tagore, this oneness was the final point of spiritual fulfilment. Tagore's highlighting of the Ultimate Reality was also a way for him to point at the civilisational partnership of Man and Nature. As such, he saw the spiritualising principle of human consciousness in its act of hospitality towards Nature. According to Tagore, humanity ought to readjust the course of human civilisation in the direction of love and fellowship. Tagore wrote:

> Our wisdom lies not in destroying separateness of units, but in maintaining the spirit of unity in its full strength [...]. Civilization has turned into a vast catering establishment It maintains constant feasts for a whole population of gluttons. The intemperance which could have been

---

6 Ibid., p. 236.

7 Ibid., p. 237.

8 Quoted in Quayum, Mohammad A., *Rabindranath Tagore: Selected Short Stories*, Introduction, New Delhi: McMillan, 2011, p. xxxvii.

> tolerated in a few has spread to the multitude. The resulting universal greed is the cause of the meanness, cruelty and lies in politics and commerce that vitiate the whole human atmosphere. A civilization with an unnatural appetite must feed on numberless victims, and these are being sought in the parts of the world where human flesh is cheap. The happiness of entire peoples in Asia and Africa is being sacrificed to provide fastidious fashion with an endless train of respectable rubbish.[9]

Tagore extended the idea of the living flow of universal humanity and his emphasis on the blossoming of the personality as a creative attempt to underline the power of love for all living beings. Consequently, he did not see the truth of the world in "the mass of materials, but their universal relatedness."[10] And he would add:

> When we know this world as alien to us then we know it as a thing mechanical, built by a divine mechanic or by a chance combination of blind forces. Then our relation to it becomes the relation of utility, and we set up our own machines or mechanical methods to deal with it and make as much profit as our knowledge of its mechanism allows us to do [...]. For us the highest purpose of this world is not merely living in it, knowing it and making use of it, but realizing our own selves in it through expansion of sympathy; not alienating ourselves from it and dominating it, but comprehending and uniting it with us in blissful union.[11]

Tagore's ideal of unity of Man and Nature deepens the former's sentiment of completeness and marks the moral progression of civilization.

Rabindranath's ecological awareness marked its highest level of intellectual maturity in the Tagorean idea of education. Tagore's ideal of education had the goal to help the individuals to be self-aware and think freely. What Tagore had in mind was to fight against uniformity and commercialism through education and prepare the individual to struggle against the spirit of greed and conquest of the universe. As he spelt it out in his essay "The

9 Tagore, Rabindranath, *The Sky of Indian History: Themes and Thoughts of Rabindranath Tagore*, Compiled and edited by S. Jeyaseela Stephen, New Delhi: UBS Publishers, 2010, pp. 229, 231.

10 Tagore, Rabindranath, "Construction verses Creation," in *Lectures and Addresses*, Madras: Macmillan, 1950, p. 61.

11 Tagore, Rabindranath, The *Sky of Indian History: Themes and Thoughts of Rabindranath Tagore*, Compiled and edited by S. Jeyaseela Stephen, New Delhi: UBS Publishers, p. 136.

Problem of Education": "If we at all understand the needs of the present day, we must see that any new schools founded by us fulfill the following conditions: that the courses are both lively and varied, and nourish the heart as well as the intellect; that no disunity or discord disrupts the minds of our young; and that education does not become something unreal, heavy and abstract with which the pupils are concerned only for those few hours when they are at school."[12] Tagore believed in holistic child development and that is why Nature and ecological awareness were among the basic components of Tagore's theory of education. Tagore's efforts towards a spirit of inclusivity and bio-pluralism were inspired by the ancient model of ashram schools, where children could learn harmony and empathy with natural diversity.

Tagore's severe critique of the mainstream schools in colonial India was also mainly due to his total rejection of what he called "factory-model" schools. Tagore argued:

> What we now call a school in this country is really a factory, and the teachers are part of it. At half-past ten in the morning the factory opens with the ringing of the bell; then, as the teachers starts talking, the machines start working. The teachers stop talking at four in the afternoon when the factory closes, and the pupils then go home carrying with them a few pages of machine-made learning. Later, this learning is tested at examinations and labelled. One advantage of a factory is that it can make goods exactly to order. Moreover, the goods are easy to label, because there is not much difference between what the different machines turn out. [...] The schools are little better than factories for turning out robots.[13]

Tagore's ecologically oriented philosophy of education sought to educate the individual in the spirit of learning from life and Nature and in opposition to all forms of machine-made learning. Tagore strongly believed in teaching children to be in touch with the world. In a lecture delivered in the United States, titled "My School", he declared: "We rob the child of his earth to teach him geography, of language to teach him grammar. His hunger is for the Epic, but he is supplied with chronicles of facts and dates. He was born in the human world, but is banished into the world of living gramophones, to expiate for the original sin of being born in ignorance. Child-nature protests

---

12 Tagore, Rabindranath, "The Problem of Education," in *Towards Universal Man*, New Delhi: Asia Publishing House, 1961, pp. 68–69.

13 Tagore, Rabindranath, "The Problem of Education," in *Towards Universal Man*, New Delhi: Asia Publishing House, 1961, pp. 67, 68.

against such calamity with all its power of suffering, subdued at last into silence by punishment."[14]

Tagore considered Nature's function "to impart the peace of the eternal to human emotions".[15] He wanted all human beings to develop empathy, friendship, and love with the world. He said: "In love all the contradictions of existence merge themselves and are lost. Only in love are unity and duality not at variance [...] In love, loss and gain are harmonized [...] Love is what brings together and inseparably connects both the act of abandoning and that of receiving."[16] Tagore interpreted love as the meeting point between the human and the divine. In his poetry volume, *Stray Birds*, he wrote: "God kisses the finite in His love and man the Infinite."[17] Therefore, either as a poet or a philosopher, Tagore was in search of a perfect unity with the living world. He continuously talked about "the world of life" in his writings, including in his most famous book of poetry, *Gitanjali*. He wrote:

> The same stream of life that runs through my veins night and day runs through the world and dances in rhythmic measures.
>
> It is the same life that shoots in joy through the dust of the earth in numberless blades of grass and breaks into tumultuous waves of leaves and flowers.
>
> It is the same life that is rocked in the ocean-cradle of birth and of death, in ebb and in flow.
>
> I feel my limbs are made glorious by the touch of this world of life.
>
> And my pride is from the life-throb of ages dancing in my blood this moment.[18]

Tagore objected to a human existence based on greed and pride. He believed that without the spiritual and natural, humankind could not discover the secrets of the universe and live in friendship and cooperation with the living world. For him, only affinity with life and living beings could open the doors of our consciousness to the secrets of the biosphere. This could only happen in the absence of violence and the mechanization of life. In a speech delivered in 1938 at Oxford, he underlined once again: "In an era of mounting anguish and vanishing worth, when disaster is fast overtaking countries and

14 Tagore, Rabindranath, *Personality*, Delhi: Macmillan India, 1980, p. 116.

15 Tagore, Rabindranath, *Creative Unity*, London: Macmillan, 1962, p. 51.

16 Tagore, Rabindranath, *Sadhana: The Realisation of Life*, London: Filiquarian Publishing, 2006, p. 90.

17 Tagore, Rabindranath, *Stray Birds*, New York: Macmillan & Co., 1916, poem no.303, p. 431.

18 Tagore, Rabindranath, *Gitanjali*, LXIX, Delhi: Macmillan, 1966, p. 63.

continents, with savagery let loose and brutal thirst for possession augmented by science, it may sound merely poetic to speak of an emergency principle of world-wide relationship [...]. But times' violence, however immediately threatening, is circumscribed, and we who live beyond it and dwell also in the larger reality of Time, must renew our faith in the permanent growth of civilization towards an ultimate purpose."[19]

Tagore was a highly eco-friendly and intercultural author. He was never willing to compromise his ideal of dialogue of civilisations for any form of nationalism. He also believed that any form of violence practised against a living being would compromise the unity of life. He affirmed: "I refuse to waste my manhood in lighting fires of anger and spreading it from house to house."[20] These arguments add up to show Tagore's attitude towards self-awareness, mutual fellowship, and inclusivism. Tagore's cosmic fellowship and philosophical holism considered the grand harmony of Nature and the kaleidoscopic picture of life. Being a pluralist at heart, he could not understand or accept the rationale behind the arrogance and cruelty of human beings towards animals and plants. Unlike the ego-centred Cartesian approach to knowledge and life, Tagore invited his readers to be guided by the freedom from the ego and the unity of truth. In his essay, "The World of Art", he observed: "Our consciousness being freed from the tangle of self-interest, we gain an unobstructed vision of unity, the incarnation of the real which is a joy forever. As in the world of art, so in God's world, our soul waits for its freedom from the ego to reach that disinterested joy which is the source and goal of creation."[21]

Tagore made no distinction between the East and the West. It was his deep conviction that one could not exist without the other. However, this was not just a cultural or political attitude that Tagore wrote broadly about. It undoubtedly followed his deep belief in the interdependence of Man and Nature. The Tagorean East-West synthesis carried with it a severe critique of materialistic civilisation and its public motto of harmonious unity with life in general. Many philosophers of the East and the West believed in the ecological message of Tagore and in his message of wisdom for humanity. In his philosophical autobiography, Hermann Keyserling, who was a close friend of Tagore, depicted a better picture of Tagore as the environmentalist, who

19 Quoted in Dutta, Krishna, Andrew Robinson, *Rabindranath Tagore: The Myriad Minded Man*, London: Bloomsbury, 1995, p. 353.

20 Tagore, Rabindranath, *Letters to a Friend: Rabindranath Tagore's Letters to C.F. Andrews*, New Delhi: Rupa, 2002, pp. 72–73.

21 Tagore, Rabindranath, *The Religion of Man*, Boston: Beacon Press, 1966, p. 184.

through his art and poetry, brought humankind closer to Nature. Hermann Keyserling celebrated Rabindranath Tagore in the following terms:

> Let me now talk about the one poet who has meant so much, immeasurably much, to me: Rabindranath Tagore. He was a creative person like the old bards and skalds who, as mentioned in the Finnish legend, first sang the forests and stars into being [...]. Once in Darmstadt Tagore told me with a sigh: "I write poetry in the same way that the trees flower in India, year in and year out. But their blossoms fall to the ground and turn to dust. Mine are collected, and that, perhaps, is not good." For the greater part of his life Tagore wrote one poem after another and composed for these one musical score after another. These songs he sang for himself. Listeners came and went; in India no doors are closed, for no visitor would intrude on a revered man. Whoever heard a single poem recited by the master never forgot it. They returned in silent contemplation and spread the poem among the people. Soon millions were singing it. In this way through his words and songs, Tagore actually created the Bengali people, and indeed possibly the future people of India. How he recited in his mother-tongue! He was then totally absorbed by rhythm, melody and word at the same time. Every fibre of his body vibrated in unison with his mind and soul. Thanks to his tremendous presence, Tagore could be and remained an improviser, even when he was reciting the best known and highly refined texts. For example, when he recited ancient Sanskrit prayers, his living faith, his living understanding, his ardent devotion to Indian tradition breathed new life into old texts. Europe has forgotten how to recognise the primeval. This we can see from the fact that Tagore is generally judged by his "literature". Parts of his writing are certainly not of the highest quality, at any rate not his English works, for as a true poet of the people (*Volksdichter*) he is strictly bound to his mother—But who with eyes to see and ears to hear cannot see in Tagore a man of letters? [...] Tagore indeed created and sang from our roots.[22]

The "roots" that Tagore turned into poetry, literature, and music were not only civilisational but also ecological. Through his multiple creations, Tagore was trying to change our relationship with the planet. It was a great dive into that great magic entity called the universe. So we can call him an

22 Quoted in Kampchen, Martin, "Rabindranath Tagore and Hermann Keyserling: A Difficult Friendship," in *The Poet and His World: Critical Essays on Rabindranath Tagore*, edited by Mohammad A. Quayum, New Delhi: Orient BlackSwan, 2011, pp. 40–41.

"environmental prophet" who requires us to think more deeply about the ecological problems that we face in the twenty-first century. Tagore could not imagine that human beings would attain a state of destruction of Nature that they would live with ever-increasing global warming. When he was writing about natural elements, most of the populations of the East and the West were indifferent to the forests, the mountains, and the oceans. Tagore helps us to understand that Mother Earth was not always overheated, and it was not always dry land where nomads and tribes dwelled. Tagore's writings magnified moments of his encounter with Nature as a journey of his soul into a harmonious creative dimension. Tagore's intimate connections with the outside world had a profound effect on his spiritual life and nourished his noble spirit. His poems are full of a mystical approach to natural elements like the sun, moon, stars, earth, sea, river, and ocean. Describing this last element, he wrote:

> "The river—messenger of the universe.
> That brings near the Far,
> And brings, even to one's door,
> The welcome of the Unknown"[23]

Interestingly, Tagore's ethical ideals are drawn from his greater partnership with Nature. As a matter of fact, Nature can be said to have been the guiding principle for a harmonic exchange paradigm, which Tagore hoped to establish for his own time and as a model for the future of humanity. We can see this in the experience that Tagore had of the first spring flood filling the dry river bed. He wrote: "The feeling which I had was like that which a man, groping through a fog without knowing his destination, might feel when he suddenly discovers that he stands before his own house [...]. All things that had seemed like vagrant waves were revealed to my mind in relation to a boundless sea."[24] As we can see, for Tagore, every journey to Nature was also a voyage of the spirit. There were no deep romantic feelings or sentiments of exoticism in his encounters with the natural world, but consciousness of a humanist experience which feeds the sources of Beauty and Truth in Tagore's eco-philosophy. We can find the same metaphysical elements in Tagore's travelogues, in his visit to Japan. He observed:

---

23 Quoted in Samantaray, Swati, Sahadeb, Patro, "The Code of Ecomysticism in Rabindranath Tagore's Works: A Critical Appraisal," *Trames*, 2018, 22(72/67), 3, p. 319.

24 Tagore, Rabindranath, *Religion of Man*, Boston: Beacon Press, 1966, pp. 94–96.

> This morning I am looking at Nature who is standing before me dressed in a garment of brown-river with a green hem. Here I am a pure observer. This observer "I", where he to express himself in language or in formal lines, would be making literature or art [...]. So also, not only in the landscape, but what moves in thought is that observer "I". There, what he says is secondary; he who says it is the principal object. As I move about looking on the beauty of the outside world, I am also moving and looking with the eye of my mind as the stream of thoughts passes inside me. These thoughts are not bound by any thread of necessity, the stream does not flow logically, but its impetus and direction spring from that same "I" [...] The greatest mystery of the world is not the thing that is seen, but the man who is seeing. An unresolvable mystery: the man tries to see himself *through* the things seen, tries to see himself by means of his multiple experience. Whatever is happening and whatever may happen-through all these events he tries to prove his worth, to see himself. The One in me, by passing through the Many, is ever realizing itself, its Oneness.[25]

Accordingly, what we find in Tagore's eco-philosophy is a perpetual search for the Oneness of Reality. As a result, the bliss can be experienced by human beings through a consciousness of Being or existence, which includes Nature and the living beings. After all, for Tagore, the cosmic fellowship with the world is nothing but the blissful consciousness of Being (*Sat-Chit-Anand*). Nature, thus, helps us to find the Infinite. In each of his encounters with Nature, Tagore was in search of the metaphysical essence of the Infinite. For example, Tagore planted a tree onNovember 8, 1926, near the Balaton Lake in Hungary. He wrote the following for this occasion:

> When I am no longer on this earth, my tree,
> Let the ever-renewed leaves of thy spring
> murmur to the wayfarers,
> "The poet did love while he lived"[26]

It was through such spiritual enterprises that Tagore sought to solve the great mysteries of life, like Beauty, Truth, and God. As such, eco-philosophy was for him making sense of where we are in the universe. Haunted by nihilism, Tagore sought to fill the spiritual void of his century with his ecological philosophy. In his metaphysical conception of the Universe, Nature alone

25 Tagore, Rabindranath, *A Visit to Japan*, New York: East West Institute, 1961, pp. 6–8.

26 Tagore, Rabindranath, *The Jewel that is Best: Collected Brief Poems*, New Delhi: Penguin Books India, 2011, p. 21.

is capable of ordering the world and combating the greed and individualist ambitions of human beings. Tagore's plea for the unity and harmony of life opens the shutters of our human civilisation to the Enlightenment and widens our eyes to the Infinite. After all, Tagore was a gardener of human destiny who knew well how to save the roots of the human tree in order that it begins to bear fruit. It is obvious that he did not regard life as an accident, but as unselfish joy, as opposed to excessive excitement of meaninglessness. His words during his visit to Japan in 1916 expressed well the entire expression of his inner self in relation to Nature. "Flowers, birds, the moon—with these we are not tormented by sorrow and suffering: we do not have to wallow in sentiment to see them: they do not sap our strength. Our only relation to them is through beauty and only three lines are needed to express this beauty:

> An old pond-
> Frogs jump
> Waters' sound."[27]

27 Tagore, Rabindranath, *A Visit to Japan*, New York: East West Institute, 1961, p. 70,

Part II

EXPERIMENTING WITH GREEN NON-VIOLENCE

Chapter 4

ECOLOGICAL SUSTAINABILITY: A GANDHIAN WAY OF LIFE

The presence of fundamentals of environmental aspects in Gandhian philosophy, such as village industry, self-sufficiency, decentralisation, and non-violence, has been discussed at length in Chapter 2, "Mahatma Gandhi: Non-Violence and Nature." His belief in the unity of man and the unity of all that lives lays the foundation of his notion of ecological sustainability. Gandhi's search for truth was achieved in harmony and peace with Nature. This holistic approach towards human life marked the quest for truth and non-violence as described in Chapter 2. His belief in non-violence (Ahimsa), the interconnectedness of not only humans but also non-human living species, and the sense of ethical responsibility unleashed the evolution of the Gandhian notion of ecology. Based on the Gandhian notion of ecology, this chapter constructs the concept of the Gandhian notion of ecological sustainability.

Ecology is identified as a synthetic perspective of Nature and not a fragmented reality. Haeckelian in his definition of ecology emphasised both living and non-living components of the natural world.[1] Andrewartha and Birch propagated the focus on the organism as the core of ecology in 1954.[2] Ever since the origin of human life, humans have benefited tremendously from the ecosystem in the form of food, timber, pharmaceuticals, fibre, and biomass fuel (Daily 1997).[3] In addition to the indirect benefits such as the maintenance of biodiversity and mitigation of flood and drought, the ecosystem provides intangible benefits from recreational, spiritual, and intellectual stimulation

1 https://www.caryinstitute.org/news-insights/2-minute-science/definition-ecology.

2 https://www.sci.muni.cz/botany/nekola/foe/Krebs__Charles_J._-_Ecology___the_experimental_analysis_of_distribution_and_abundance-Pearson_Education_Limited__2014_.pdf.

3 Daily, G.C., *Nature's Services: Societal Dependence on Natural Ecosystems,* Washington, DC: Island Press, 1997a.

(Postel and Carpenter 1997).[4] Thus, the benefits derived by humankind from the ecosystem are generally underappreciated (Daily 1997 b).[5] Moreover, the notion that a developing country such as India is 'too poor to be green' has been critically analysed by Ramchandra Guha (Guha, 2025).[6] Guha (2025) quoted the contemporary works of Rabindranath Tagore, Radhakamal Mukerjee, J. C. Kumarappa, Patrick Geddes, Albert and Gabrielle Howard, Mira, Verrier Elwin, K. M. Munshi, and M. Krishnan, who contributed research and literature related to wild forests, soil and water, urbanisation, and industrialisation. In contrast to the "full-stomach environmentalism", Guha contended it as a "livelihood environmentalism, asserting that their writings played a significant role in shaping the global conversations about humanity's relationship with nature."

While developing the Gandhian notion of ecological sustainability, it is crucial to examine and investigate how humankind evolved its understanding or connection with ecology. The human race has experienced uncontrolled and unprecedented consumerism, imposing extreme destruction on the bounties of nature, resources, and species. This brutal and violent act against nature was soon recognised by several philosophers from all disciplines. Moreover, the question of sustainability was contemplated more than ever before, resulting in many contesting definitions and discourses. The unprecedented production and consumption by humankind have significantly jeopardised the viability of the ecosystem (Vitousek et al. 1997).[7] Consequently, the long-term sustainability of ecosystems finds its foundation in the responsible stewardship of natural resources (Lubchenco et al. 1991).[8] In current times, the notion of ecological sustainability seeks to achieve, restore, and maintain the composition, structure, and function of ecosystems so that future generations continue to derive the same benefits. This envisages a strategic pathway for the

4 Postel, S., Carpenter, S., "Freshwater Ecosystem Services," in *Nature's Services: Societal Dependence on Natural Ecosystems,* edited by G.C. Daily, pp. 195–214, Washington, DC: Island Press.

5 Daily, G.C., "Introduction: What are Ecosystem Services?" in *Nature's Services: Societal Dependence on Natural Ecosystems,* edited by G.C. Daily, pp. 1–10, Washington, DC: Island Press, 1997b.

6 Guha, R., *Speaking with Nature: The Origins of Indian Environmentalism,* New Haven: Yale University Press, 2025.

7 Vitousek, P.M., Mooney, H.A., Lubchenco, H.A., Melillo, J.M., "Human Domination of Earth's Ecosystems," *Science,* 1997, 277, pp. 494–499.

8 Lubchenco, J., Olson, A.M., Brubaker, L.B. [and others], "The Sustainable Biosphere Initiative: An Ecological Research Agenda," *Ecology,* 1991, 72, pp. 318–325.

long-term resource consumption pattern of humankind (Dale et al., 2000).[9] This leads us to the concept of sustainable development, considering how sustainably humankind can sustain the ecosystem subject to its long-term consumption pattern.

The Gandhian notion of ecological sustainability begins fundamentally from his notion of a simple lifestyle, which remains consistent throughout his life. It is difficult to disassociate destruction from development. Considering this inevitable fact of destruction, Gandhi looks at minimising the degradation or damage that is a by-product of development. The great standard of living comes at the cost of environmental degradation and greater consumerism at the cost of over-exploitation. Both environmental degradation and over-exploitation are viewed as attributes of violence according to Gandhian philosophy.

When interviewed by a journalist, and asked whether he would like India to have the same standard of living as that of Great Britain, Gandhi replied, "That tiny country Britain had to exploit half the globe to have its standard of living. How many globes will India have to exploit?"[10] Gandhi manifested the notion of ethics in development. According to Gandhi, the meaning of development was not the accumulation of material wealth but to place nature at the centre and emphasize the "betterment of human life", ensuring the fulfilment of the basic needs of all human beings.

Gandhi's notion of sustainable development was conceived in his remarkable contribution "*Hind Swaraj*" in 1909.[11] Gandhi categorically condemned modern civilisation. According to him, modern civilisation seeks to increase bodily comforts and fails even in doing so. This civilisation has created people who lack physical strength and courage. The energy is caught up under intoxication. Humanity is moving towards self-destruction. There is no inducement of morality or religion (*Hind Swaraj*, 1938).[12]

He asserted the consequences of unprecedented consumerism and capitalism. The inherent relationship between man and nature has been destroyed ever since the onset of industrialisation. Sustainable development, according to Gandhi, was mainly to reconstruct the harmonious relationship between man and the ecosystem. It is a principle or doctrine of human existence. It is embedded in the way of life of every human, keeping man at the centre

---

9 Dale, V.H., Brown, S., Haeuber, R.A. [and others], "Ecological Principles and Guidelines for Managing the Use of Land," *Ecological Applications,* 2000, 10, pp. 639–670.

10 ile:///C:/Users/pooja%20sharma/Downloads/articles_Bindu3_feb2017%20(1).pdf.

11 Gandhi, M.K., *Hind Swaraj or Indian Home Rule,* Navjivan Publishing House, 1938.

12 Ibid.

of all activities. Gandhiji contended that human civilisation or way of life is that mode of conduct that points out to man the path of duty. According to him, performance of duty and observance of morality are convertible terms. As a result, to observe morality is to attain mastery over our minds and our passions. Thus, by doing so, we know and discover ourselves. He further added, "our mind is a restless bird, the more it gets the more it wants, and remains unsatisfied. The more we indulge our passions the more unbridled they become."

Our ancestors, therefore, set a limit to our indulgences. They saw that happiness was largely a mental condition. A man is not necessarily happy because he is rich, or unhappy because he is poor. On the contrary, the rich are often seen to be unhappy, and the poor to be happy. Millions will always remain poor. Observing all this, our ancestors dissuaded us from luxuries and pleasures. We have maintained the same kind of technology that existed thousands of years ago, the same cottages, and indigenous education. We have had no fire-corroding competition. Each member of society followed his occupation or trade and charged a regulation wage. The truth is that it is not that we did not know how to invent machinery, but our forefathers knew that if we set our hearts on such things, we would become slaves and lose moral fibre. After due deliberation, they decided that we should only do what we could with our hands and feet. They saw that our real happiness and health consisted in the proper use of our hands and feet. Machinery, according to Gandhi, was like a snake-hole. Where there is machinery there are large cities, and where there are large cities, there are tram cars and railways. Further, wherever means of artificial locomotion have increased, the health of the people has suffered.

Our forefathers conceded that the people would never be happy in large cities. The large cities would become centres of gangs of thieves and robbers, where poor men would be robbed by rich men. They were, therefore, satisfied with small villages. Moreover, they saw that kings and their swords were inferior to the swords of ethics, and therefore, sovereigns of the earth were to be inferior to the Rishis and Fakirs. A nation with these attributes is better to teach others than to learn from others. All the stakeholders, such as courts, lawyers, and doctors, performed their activities and duties well within the bounds or limits. None of them ever considered themselves superior to any of the others. Each of these stakeholders of the society never robbed the people; rather, they were people's dependents and not their masters. The justice was fair, and the tradition was to avoid courts. The people lived independently and followed agricultural occupations. Thus, such people or nations enjoyed true Home Rule.

Gandhi further added, "It is observed wherever the cursed modern civilization has not reached, India remains as it was before. People living in such regions of India, Britishers could never rule over them, nor would they ever rule over anyone. The regions belonging to the interiors have not yet been polluted by modern civilization. He further added that Indian civilization tends to elevate the moral being."

Having examined the detrimental impact of modern civilisation, as described in *Hind Swaraj*, it is imperative to redefine the phenomenon of development, as a notion of development that is more sustainable and integrates all the dimensions of the ecosystem. Such a system can be visualised by an overall shift in the way of life, mainly the process of production and consumption, the political framework, and the habits of mankind. According to Gandhi, a long-term development process that places the moral responsibility of individuals on their lifestyle, community level, national as well as international level is considered sustainable development. In this context, his doctrine of "Sarvodaya" reflects "Universal Uplift" or "Progress of All". The essence of environmental ethics was advocated through the notion of Sarvọdaya. Gandhi's vision of Sarvodaya implied preserving the harmonious existence of humankind with nature and other living beings (Tiwari, 2019).[13]

Originating from the notion of Sarvodaya, the "Trusteeship model" emerges, based on the attributes of non-possession in the state, individuals, and all stakeholders. The Trusteeship model establishes the relationship of humans with nature. Humans serve as custodians of nature and bequeath the natural resources to future generations. When human civilisation views natural resources as curators, individuals will try to restore every part of it for the future. Innovations will commence not to destroy natural treasures but to secure and protect them.

The notion of *Sarvodaya* is based on three basic principles. Firstly, that the good of the individual is contained in the good of all. Secondly, every labourer in society has the same right to earn their livelihood from their work. Finally, the life of the tiller of the soil and the handicraftsman is a life worth living.[14] Gandhiji believed that "the earth provides enough to satisfy every man's needs, but not for every man's greed". Therefore, the *Sarvodaya* society consists of every member who is free from greed for any kind of acquisition of material wealth and luxurious lifestyle. Such a society ensures adequate opportunity to produce and earn honestly to obtain a decent and respectful living. People in such a society will get earnings according to their talent, ability, and labour.

---

13 Tiwari, R.R., "Gandhi was an Environmentalist," *The Indian Journal of Medical Research*, 2019, 149(Suppl 1), p. S141.

14 https://www.mkgandhi.org/articles/gandhi_sarvodaya.html.

All earnings over and above the minimum level required for a decent and simple living will be given up for the overall good of society as a whole. All wealth and land are considered common property, to be utilised for the welfare of society. The members owning access to resources will serve as custodians of excess resources and become the trustees of excess wealth. This excess wealth is further used for the uplift of weaker sections of society. He was not against technology but favoured technology that does not destroy the bounties of nature and also the technology must not result in the concentration of power in the hands of a few.

Gandhi strongly advocated that everyone must uphold the dignity of labour irrespective of the type of honest labour performed by an individual,[15] as advocated by Leo Tolstoy. The network of such self-supporting village communities will comprise the whole village as one family. Such large village communities will be devoid of any discrimination or distinction based on race, creed, caste, or language. The agricultural and industrial activities will be planned in such a way that all the individuals in the community are employed. The governance of such a system is through the village council or a representative of the whole village.

The society based on the Gandhian notion of trusteeship and Sarvodaya will be free from the negative outcomes of the tyranny of majority rule, the absence of centralised authority, and where politics is not the instrument of power. Imbibed with the spirit of love, truth, and self-sacrifice, such a society will function based on non-violence. There is no existence of private property, and all the instruments of exploitation and social distinctions are discarded. The movement towards such a society was referred to as the Sarvodaya movement, which undertook various projects. Several leaders, such as Vinoba Bhave, J. P. Narayan, Dharmadhikari, and Dhirendra Mazumdar, undertook many projects, including Bhoodan and Gramdan movements in the 1950s and 1960s.[16] Based on the fundamentals of the good of all, the rich and the poor will give up all their attachment to private property and will continue to work for the good of all. These attributes are bound to limit greed and distinguish between wants and desires, redefining ethical wants. Thus, a harmonious existence of mankind and nature rests on the coexistence of all cultures and civilizations.

Gandhi's epic work, *Hind Swaraj* explicitly criticised modern civilization and highlighted how it tremendously hampered adherence to moralities

---

15 Gokhale, B.K., *Political Science* (Theory & Govt. Machinary), Himalaya Publishing House, 1960.

16 https://www.mkgandhi.org/articles/gandhi_sarvodaya.html.

and the exercise of restraint. In 1911, Gandhi used the phrase "Economy of Nature," bringing about a sensitivity and deeper understanding of human actions and ecology. Gandhi's every action or thought undertaken was a reflection of minimizing wants (Pathak and Pal, 2020).[17] The famous Dandi Yatra of 1930 was motivated by the right of the common man over natural resources. Salt, being a primary natural resource, became a significant part of the independence movement. The broad objective of the whole movement was "freeing the world from the detrimental greed of materialism". The mindless consumption of natural resources became the reason for unsustainable modern civilisation. Gandhiji demonstrated the minimisation of wants when someone brought oranges for him on a motorcycle, which he refused to accept, saying that when you can walk, avoid the motorcycle.

The present era is confronted with the problem of water scarcity and lack of safe drinking water, owing to declining water levels and deforestation. However, 60 years back, Gandhi asked for tree plantation and suggested water harvesting for irrigational purposes to avoid famines and food shortages. Inspired by Gandhian thoughts on the environment, Germany established the Green Party. One of the founders of the party admired the impact of Mahatma, stating, "In the particular area of our work we have been greatly inspired by Mahatma Gandhi, that is, in our belief that lifestyle and method of production, which relies on the endless supply of raw materials from other parties. In contrast, responsible consumption of raw materials as a part of ecologically oriented lifestyle and economy reduces the risk that policies of violence will be pursued." Thus, policies consistent with nature preservation were pursued.

For sustainability to be achieved, the socioeconomic, political, and ecological concepts are put together to address all the environmental challenges. Further, ecological sustainability pertains to analysing the systematic relationship between plants and animals and their habitat and environment. Placing humans at the centre of all relationships, ecological sustainability calls for the responsibility of human beings to maintain and preserve the interlinkages between man, nature, and other living and non-living entities. This, in turn, calls for the consistent, active participation of all the members of society. It needs the inner transformation of all individuals in the society, taking them away from the clutches of greed, selfishness, sense of ownership, and accumulation of wealth. A change in attitude that accommodates all the living and non-living entities in nature, and distinguishes between ethical

---

17 Pathak, H., Pal, S., Mohapatra, T., *Mahatma Gandhi's Vision of Agriculture Achievements of ICAR*, Indian Council of Agricultural Research, 2020.

means and values the importance of means over the ends. The Gandhian notion of ecological sustainability is a spiritually oriented, holistic approach.

An environmentally conscious individual will make ethical choices in daily life such as energy-conserving habits, saving water, choosing food, clothes, and travel, and so on. The spirit of saving the environment, in turn, will evolve individuals as humans. Gandhi's notion of Sarvodaya, "welfare of all", which is a community-centred approach, will ensure the betterment of human life. His philosophy takes us from "survival of the fittest" to making everyone fit to survive. His ideology leads us towards "Absolute Truth".

The emphasis on non-use value, the altruistic value assigned to goods, is a strategic reflection of the missing fundamentals of Gandhian thought in economics. The emerging focus on "Biocentrism", an ethical view that extends equal value to all living things, is a welcoming development in understanding ecological sustainability from a Gandhian perspective. Biocentrism conceives that humans' lives are no more valuable than any other living organisms and that all living things should be given equal priority to humans when it comes to ethical and moral decisions.[18]

Later, the book *Surviving the Century: Facing Climate Chaos* by Prof. Herbert Girardet, gives the concept of an "Earth community". His concept of an Earth community is based on the fundamentals of Gandhian philosophy: "Earth has enough resources for everybody's needs and not for anybody's greed."[19] Later in 2007, *Time* magazine quoted 51 global warming survival guides (Global Warming Survival Guide, April 9, 2007).[20] The 51st guide recommends sharing more and consuming less for a simplified life. In other words, we can learn to live simply so that others can simply live.

For Gandhi, the notion of sustainability is largely the harmonious coexistence of mankind and nature. This interconnectedness of humans with nature is based not only on equity and justice but also on the coexistence of all cultures along with the existing ecosystem. His initiative and endeavour of the Dandi March of 1930 is the epitome of asserting the right of every person over the essential, limited resources of nature. Therefore, his statement that "Earth has enough resources for everybody's needs but not for anybody's greed", has become a universal truth and a solution to all challenges of today's world. By this statement, Gandhi wanted every individual to realise the detrimental

18 Bari, Judi, Revolutionary Ecology: Biocentrism & Deep Ecology," *Alarm: A Journal of Revolutionary Ecology,* 1995.

19 Girardet, H., ed., *Surviving the Century: Facing Climate Chaos and Other Global Challenges,* Routledge, 2012.

20 https://content.time.com/time/covers/0,16641,20070409,00.html.

effects of the accumulation and possession of unlimited wealth and letting them free themselves from the clutches of materialism and consumerism.

For ethical consumption, Gandhi proposed the ideology of means and ends and distinguishing wants from desires. The notion of means and ends holds a phenomenal significance in the goal of ecological sustainability. The interconnection between means and ends is more ethical than technical. He emphasised that evil or violent means will never lead to good ends. His notion of means and ends is similar to that of a seed and a tree, signifying the close connection between the two. He contends that the end lies in the means just as the tree lies within the seed. He insists that we have control over the means but not over the end; he believes that we essentially reap what we sow. He recognises that impure means would lead to impure ends; truth cannot be attained through untruthful means, and justice cannot be secured through unjust means. Finally, the notion of ends can never justify means and therefore, the moral means is an end in itself since the virtue is its reward.

Having emphasised the role of means in the Gandhian philosophy of life, the everyday activity of humans must comply with each means selected to secure any end. A life based on fair means is bound to lead to a sustainable path towards the goal. Consequently, the discourse of means and end has significant implications for achieving sustainable goals in contemporary times. The Sustainable Development Goals, as identified by the United Nations, are best realised by the philosophy of means and ends as advocated by Gandhian thoughts. The sustainability of goals rests in the means or the pathways to achieve the goals. The truth of the sustainable goals lies in the policy pathways to achieve these goals. In other words, the notion of sustainable development envisages climate action under the Sustainable Development Goal, SDG 13. This goal calls for strengthening resilience and adaptive capacity to climate-related hazards and natural disasters and integrating climate change measures into national policies, strategies, and planning. However, while achieving that end, the policies adopted render certain sections of society towards poverty and hunger, depriving them of equal opportunity as a consequence of the political economy of the state. Such policies or means are considered evil or detrimental to the larger goal.

One can say that ecological sustainability can only be realised by living a day-to-day life most sustainably, and not by fragmenting the pathways independently. Since each of the SDGs is interconnected, the choice of the means to attain the one common goal of ecological sustainability is crucial. The more ethical, apolitical, and selfless (devoid of vested interests) the policies or means adopted are, the more chances there are that we are drawn closer to the Truth of the goal.

Gandhian philosophy of sustainability emerges from the self-realisation of truth, when people realise individual responsibility for their own lives and take control of their destiny. While doing that, they not only comprehend the significance and role of nature but also take initiatives for a peaceful coexistence with living and non-living entities. The notion of sustainability is embedded in the day-to-day activity of human life, the way humans consume, produce commodities, and use resources to meet their demands. Every day, the demand created by an individual is the reflection of their level of self-realization of truth. The means adopted by individuals to meet or achieve that demand is also a reflection of how they conceived the whole philosophy of non-violent existence and "economy of permanence".

Another concept of "economy of permanence" based on Gandhian philosophy is a contribution by J. C. Kumarappa (Kumarappa, 1946).[21] The concept is comparable to the lines of "the cradle-to-cradle" philosophy, generating lesser wastage and using renewable sources in production processes (Bakker, et. Al, 2020).[22] The concept of permanence is absolute, beyond Time and Space. Such a concept of permanence could be attributed to God, Truth, and Love that are unchangeable. Within the gambit of Time and Space, nothing is permanent. For Gandhi, Nature was analogous to God. However, when Nature is not considered God and is understood as limited by Time and Space, then nature could strike through in the future. In this context, human life is said to be Transient compared to that of Nature, which is Permanent.[23] This philosophy reinforces the individual to adopt a lifestyle guided by the individual responsibility that arises from the essence of the continuity of life.

Gandhi himself led an essentially non-violent life, respecting nature and its creations. He advocated conscious efforts to use the resources of nature to the bare minimum in an attempt to conserve natural resources even if they were available in abundance. He propagated a lifestyle that was absolutely in tune with nature, a lifestyle that allowed everyone to satisfy their wants equally without discrimination and use the resources to the least possible extent. He believed that man could not exploit nature infinitely to satisfy his unlimited wants, thus propagating the notion of an "economy of permanence".

Gandhi believed that "God manifests himself in innumerable forms in this universe and every such manifestation commands my spontaneous respect."

21 Kumarappa, Joseph Cornelius, *The Economy of Permanence*, Delhi: Maganvadi, 1946.

22 Bakker, C.A., Wever, R., Teoh, C., De Clercq, S., "Designing Cradle-to-cradle Products: A Reality Check," *International Journal of Sustainable Engineering*, 2010, 3(1), pp. 2–8.

23 https://www.emerald.com/insight/content/doi/10.1108/978-1-83753-380-020231010/full/html?skipTracking=true.

He insisted on the concepts of limitation of wants and the notion that simplicity has great ecological significance. He believed in the oneness of life; all creation, both living and non-living, are so closely interdependent that one cannot harm the other without harming oneself. This notion even surpasses the notion of "Pareto optimality", defined in welfare economics. The branch of welfare economics that attempted to capture the welfare of all individuals in society formulated the concept of Pareto optimality, which is defined as a state in which resources are optimised in a manner that any movement away from this state will make at least one person worse off without making any person better off.[24] This notion of welfare optimality ignored the existence of the environment and the interconnectedness of humans with the environment. In the Gandhian framework, the optimality or harmony is achieved not only inside the human mind and body as well as among humans, but also between humans and the environment surrounding them. It is the attainment of harmony with universal Truth, the Ultimate Reality, and it is this harmony that sustains through life and beyond life.

Thus, the protection and preservation of nature becomes the moral responsibility of all of humanity. Everything in the universe is a manifestation of the Ultimate and therefore every object in Nature is highly evolved and possesses great dignity inherited from the Ultimate. Consequently, every creation must be treated with reverence.[25] In addition, the harmony imbibed in the individual mind, body, and soul is bound to translate itself into the living and non-living entities in their surroundings. Any disequilibrium within the harmony of mind, body, and soul will affect the interpersonal relationship between the living and non-living. Any disproportionate growth of any entity, neglecting the welfare of others, will hamper the harmonious evolution of sustainable development in a true sense. As a result, the best choice is that human beings must consider themselves as the custodians of the bounties of nature and make efforts to protect and preserve them. Thus, humanity must strive to achieve a balance between lifestyle, nature, and the ultimate Truth.

The Gandhian philosophy condemns overproduction and unsustainable consumerism, which has detrimental consequences on the environment. He advocates an alternative framework for development that will ensure sustainable development. In Gandhi's development paradigm, consumerism is discarded while conservation is adopted. Mass production is replaced by production for the masses, private ownership is replaced by community ownership and common goods, and centralised governance is substituted by

24 https://www.sciencedirect.com/topics/engineering/pareto-optimality.
25 https://www.mkgandhi.org/articles/ecology.html.

decentralised systems.[26] The Gandhian paradigm of sustainable development is based on the ethical and moral transformation of an individual. It is a journey of enlightenment that embarks the sustainability in the way one perceives life itself.

In the present world, the notion of sustainable development has evolved in a very contestable manner. The presence of almost 40 definitions of the term "sustainable development" in the Blueprint for Green Economy,[27] is itself evidence of this discourse. The most widely used definition evolved in the Brundtland Report: "Sustainable development is the development that meets the needs of the present without compromising the ability of future generations to meet their own needs" (WCED, 1987).[28] The spectrum of sustainable development pertains to larger dimensions than just the notion of traditional environmentalism. The concept incorporates the components of social, economic, and ecological relevance.

Before the notion of sustainable development, the term Corporate Social Responsibility (CSR) was coined in 1953 by an American economist Howard Bowen, referred to as the father of CSR. In his book, *Social Responsibilities of the Businessman*, he signifies the role of corporates and the impact of their actions on society. He asserted that businessmen were obliged to pursue policies for the common good. The term refers to "business self-regulation to be socially accountable", and being socially accountable involves reducing carbon footprints, improving working conditions, and recognising the duty towards the world (Casey Scoff, 2024).[29] Thus, the components of sustainable and inclusive investment processes were incorporated.

The notion or practice of ESG evolved in the 1960s as socially responsible investing, incorporating environmental, social, and governance dimensions. This concept mainly evolved in Western societies, and its dimensions have advanced over time. In 2004, the United Nations report, "Who Cares Wins", contained a substantial mention of ESG in the present context. Gradually, the components of SDGs have been incorporated into millennium development goals to promote peaceful and inclusive societies for sustainable development, provide access to justice for all, and build effective, accountable, and inclusive institutions at all levels. Later, guided by the urgency to combat climate crises, along with environmental laws, the sustainability issue became the

26 https://www.mkgandhi.org/articles/ecology.html.

27 Barbier, E.B., "Blueprint for a Green Economy David Pearce, Anil Markandya and," in *The Top 50 Sustainability Books*, pp. 70–76, Routledge, 2017.

28 WCED, *Our Common Future*, 1st ed., Oxford: Oxford University Press, 1987, p. 44.

29 https://www.ecolytics.io/blog/evolution-of-csr.

leading driver of all agendas of international summits such as COP26. This was the journey of the evolution of sustainable development in the present world.

However, the world has not yet come closer to the notion of ecological sustainability as propagated by the Gandhian perspective. The sustainable development goals are sustainable only with the moral and ethical pathways adopted by the policymakers. This is the strong message being conveyed by the Gandhian philosophy of "means and end". Each SDG is interconnected with the others and thus serves a single purpose of ecological sustainability. The underlying connection between SDGs makes it essential to perceive the indivisibility of all challenges and the comprehensive solution to resolve them. When the means to resolve the present challenges shared by humanity as a whole originate from the purity of thought or Truth, the end will attain its destiny of Truth.

Chapter 5

ASHRAMS OF GANDHI IN INDIA AND ABROAD: EPITOME OF SUSTAINABILITY

Gandhi's fundamental belief in the interconnectedness between Man and Nature was immensely reflected in the way of life or day-to-day routine of individuals in the society. Gandhi's notion of sustainability was based on ethical and moral transformation within the individuals themselves. This journey of enlightenment that individuals experience bears the seeds of sustainability. Further, this process of learning and living envisages humanity striking a balance between lifestyle, nature, and the ultimate Truth. Chapter 4 demonstrated how the means to resolve the present challenges shared by humanity as a whole originate from the purity of thought or Truth, and the end will attain its destiny of Truth.

The philosophy advocated by Gandhi was not an idealised hypothetical framework but an integrated and comprehensive model that endures practical applications. The ashrams of Gandhi are living examples of practical demonstrations of his philosophy. The journey of self-transformation, which is the underlying principle of Gandhian philosophy, traversed both the inner and outer worlds. It was never independent of the community, society, and ecology around it. This journey of inner evolution towards sustainable pathways of living could practically evolve in perfectly designed ashrams that operated on Gandhian principles. These ashrams were the roots of sustainable living, fostering harmony among humans and between humans and nature.

This method of collective living aims to achieve one objective: peaceful and sustainable living, based on the fundamental notion of interconnectedness between every living and non-living entity of nature. This underlying principle of interconnectedness becomes the basis of everyday activity in the community. Every activity is systematically linked to attaining self-transformation and uplift towards ethical and moral values. The activities in the ashrams revolve around sustainable agricultural practices, adopting organic ways of growing vegetables, and conserving resources such as water.

All such activities promote and foster individual skills and effectively deploy environmentally sustainable technology, conserving resources.

The ashrams of Gandhi served as experimental laboratories for a non-violent, alternative way of living.[1] These ashrams later became the epitome of peace, harmony, self-renunciation, and constructive work. The ashrams were small communities that practised the principles of Truth and non-violence. Gandhi's first two ashrams were founded in South Africa, during the time he lived there from 1893 to 1914. The first settlement, Phoenix Settlement, was established in 1904 in KwaZulu Natal, and the other, Tolstoy Farm was established in 1910 outside Johannesburg. The other two ashrams were founded in India when he returned to the country in 1915. The first ashram in India was Sabarmati Ashram, established in 1915 outside Ahmedabad, and Sevagram Ashram, established in 1936 in Wardha.

In the two ashrams in India, Gandhi aimed at commencing a counter-world, where the inhabitants engaged in a lifestyle based on self-control and harmony with the pursuit of spiritual uplift and liberation.[2] Each of the residents of the ashram was consistently engaged in the act of community work and service. The residents of the ashram tilled the soil together, cooked meals together, spun clothes together, and cleaned the toilets, breaking all the barriers of caste, gender, race, and religion. They practised non-violence and harmony all the time and inculcated the moral pursuit of truth, satyagraha. The ashrams reflected a consolidated community demonstrating complete civic responsibility.

Gandhi was highly influenced by the ideas of Tolstoy concerning religion, renunciation, voluntary poverty, community, and vegetarianism. The Tolstoyan idea of cooperative communities had a significant influence on Gandhi, and it is reflected substantially in Hind Swaraj. Tolstoy's notion of non-violence was transcended to the next level by Gandhi by conceiving the term *satyagraha* (the truth force). He believed that non-violence could suggest a negative form of action, while passive resistance could be associated with the defence of the weak, but satyagraha is considered an instrument of spirituality and morally strong. The practice of satyagraha is not only an active refusal to commit a violent action, but the will to suffer and serve selflessly to convert the opposition. Thus, Tolstoy's notion of "self-suffering" as a means of humanising society was further refined by Gandhi.

The writings of Ruskin and Thoreau further inspired Gandhi and reinforced his belief in self-renunciation and respect for the dignity of the

---

1 https://egyankosh.ac.in/bitstream/123456789/63923/1/Block-4.pdf.

2 http://enhancinglife.uchicago.edu/blog/the-legacy-of-gandhis-ashrams.

individual. Thus, he believed that in the democratic society of Gandhi's vision, the individual is given priority, but if the all-round development of the individual is to be valued then it could be realised in the society by the freedom and welfare of all the members of the society.

Gandhi read "*Unto This Last*", in 1904 and remarked, "It captured me and made me transform life."[3] Based on the notions of the "Phoenix Settlement in Natal" and Ruskin's philosophy, he concluded three fundamental principles. First, the good of the individual is contained in the good of all. Secondly, the right to earn a livelihood is the same for everyone. Thirdly, the life of labour is worth living; in other words, the life of the tiller of the soil and the life of a handicraftsman are lives worth living. The alternative model proposed by Ruskin was not to achieve greater wealth but simpler pleasure. Gandhi shared his complete understanding and concerns about the quality of life and discontent with material accumulation.

When Gandhi reached South Africa, the desire to experiment with communal living envisaged the type of community he visualized.[4] A micro-community that lived based on voluntary poverty, self-renunciation, and constructive work. Inspired by Ruskin, Gandhi attempted to reorient his life based on simplicity and self-sufficiency in Durban in 1897. A simple life for him meant reducing expenditure by washing his clothes and cutting his hair. Life in the Phoenix Settlement in Natal became the first experiment in 1904 based on Ruskin's *Unto This Last.*[5] A simple life based on love, labour, and the dignity of human beings became the centre stage of all alternative ways of living. An extensive examination of the Gita made him realise that the attribute of non-possession meant that seeking salvation would imply becoming "trustees" of the community. Later, it took the shape of the "Trusteeship" model propagated by Gandhi.

Such a community that was visualised had its printing press, a flour mill worked by water power, and an oil press. All men worked in the fields, which grew a variety of tropical fruits and vegetables. The community largely reflected a multi-racial community devoid of tensions and prejudices. Gandhi further argued that the value system based on Truth and non-violence could only be visualised if social workers and politicians all accepted self-sacrifice

3 Woodcock, George, *Anarchism*, Middlesex: Penguin Books, 1963, p. 24.

4 Thomas, Mark, *Gandhi and His Ashrams*, Mumbai, India: Popular Prakashan Pvt. Ltd., 1993, p. 42. https://www.mkgandhi.org/ebks/Gandhi_and_his_Ashrams.pdf.

5 https://www.mkgandhi.org/articles/surendrabhana.php#:~:text=The%20Tolstoy%20Farm%20was%20the,the%20dignity%20of%20human%20beings.

in both personal and public life.[6] The Indian Vedic system of education advocated forest retreats where teachers and students lived a life of restraint and spiritual discipline. Gandhi's notion of ashram life was similar to the Vedic ideal but not limited to personal development; it also advocated all services undertaken in the cause of community and national development.

The ashram life advocated a lifestyle that enabled individuals to live in harmony not only with fellow humans but also with nature, thus propagating the notion of ecological sustainability. Self-reliance, creativity, and community service were the attributes emphasised by such a living. Such a community propagated collective living, constructive activity, and simple living. Gandhi's ideas overlapped with those of Walden Thoreau who clearly stated that humans cannot realise their full potential in a material life and passive acceptance of violence and oppression. To evolve as human beings, they have to strive on the path of non-violence, simplicity, and truth.[7]

In 1910, Tolstoy Farm was established based on Phoenix Settlement. It was a cooperative movement, a community where satyagrahis and their families would support themselves.[8] They would live a simple life in harmony with one another and with nature. Inculcating the spirit of cooperation as it was in the Phoenix Settlement, the community at Tolstoy Farm emphasised communal living, sharing accommodation, and cultivating the entire land collectively. The objective was to cultivate jointly to ensure the efficient production of larger crops. In the communities that Gandhi established, the lifestyle was rural-oriented, non-exploitative, and based on the dignity of labour. This notion mainly envisaged that if all men only strive for self-sufficiency by performing enough labour to produce daily needs, their wants will be minimized. People would aim to eat to live rather than live to eat.

The preliminary requirement to run the Tolstoy farm was the opportunity to experiment with the implementation of novel ideas and thoughts. Gandhi believed that an individual's life was meant for self-realisation with experiments. The self-realisation comes from the search for Truth, more specifically the absolute Truth as the ultimate reality.[9] An individual must strive to discover what truth means for him and practice it in life with single-mindedness. Truth can also be explained as "soul force". According to Gandhi, soul force

---

6 Quoted in Gandhi, M.K., *Hind Swaraj*, Ahmedabad: Navajivan Publishing House, 1938, pp. 131–132; cf. Iyer, op. cit., p. 271.

7 Thomas, Mark, *Gandhi and His Ashrams*, Mumbai, India: Popular Prakashan Pvt. Ltd., 1993, p. 36. https://www.mkgandhi.org/ebks/Gandhi_and_his_Ashrams.pdf.

8 Ibid., 76.

9 https://www.mkgandhi.org/articles/surendrabhana.php#:~:text=The%20Tolstoy%20Farm%20was%20the,the%20dignity%20of%20human%20beings.

is the use of the permanent and superior nature of the soul. This force is infinitely superior to physical force when the motive is to address anything wrong.

To realise the soul force, certain principles needed to be observed by the satyagrahis. In 1916, certain principles were laid down to accomplish the attainment of Truth or Satya. He was aware of the rich cultural heritage of Hindu tradition; therefore, much influenced by Hindu religious ideology, he laid down certain principles. The first was the principle of ahimsa, implying non-violence. The second principle was asetya, meaning non-stealing, non-covetousness. The third principle was aparigraha, implying non-possession and non-acquisitiveness and the fourth principle was brahmacharya, meaning practicing celibacy, an attribute emphasised in Hindu religion essential for moral growth and uplift.

However, there exists no evidence regarding these principles being formally laid down by the residents of Tolstoy Farm. Gandhi believed that these principles would encourage the kind of value system that would bring the required transformation among the satyagrahis. The process of self-realisation and self-transformation is a continuum process and it requires effort each day. Daily life in the ashram must reflect the new order or phenomenon necessary to realise the transformation.

Gandhi wanted to cultivate among the residents of Tolstoy Farm those virtues which he considered high in his own life. Most of the time, he did not propagate these highly valued virtues through lectures or by communicating their positive impact on life; rather, his charismatic presence itself was so powerful that demanded individuals to enquire more about the ethical and moral underpinning behind the principles set forth by the ashram. Where logic failed, Gandhi's aura and enigmatic persona played a part in transforming individuals from the core.

The rural region played a significant role in the Gandhian perception of life and ashrams. The fundamental virtue of a simple life could only originate from the rural setting. A human could tap his full potential only by living closer to nature. The presence of open spaces, trees, and fruits provided residents with a huge opportunity for farming and gardening. Such activities engaged all the members with some sort of interaction with nature or the other.

When Gandhi returned in India in 1914, he received overwhelming love. Gandhi met Gopal Krishna Gokhale and shared his vision of establishing an ashram. But he promised Gokhale to travel across India before starting

Satyagraha in India (Madras Courier, January 8, 2024).[10] The first ashram in India was established at Kochrab village in Paldi near Ahmedabad in 1915 after he returned from South Africa. The original name of the ashram was "Satyagraha" ashram, also known as "Kochrab Ashram". Sevashram was another name given to it, implying "the abode of service". Since the purpose was the devotion to the truth, the name selected was "Satyagraha Ashram"; this name communicated both the goal and the method adopted to achieve the goal. The ashram at Sabarmati became home to Gandhi from 1917 to 1930. The ashram later witnessed many pivotal movements such as the Non-cooperation Movement and Dandi March. The Satyagraha Ashram at Kochrab in 1915 was shifted to Sabarmati Ashram located on the banks of the river Sabarmati in 1917. In Sabarmati Ashram, Gandhi embarked on several experiments such as spinning and weaving, and khadi evolved as a symbol of economic liberation. The experiments in education led to the establishment of Gujarat Vidyapith in 1920.[11] The teachers of Gujarat Vidyapith were urged to adopt a village and educate people.

The Sabarmati Ashram, also known as Harijan Ashram, became the centre of all movements of the Indian freedom struggle. The Ashram was originally referred to as "Satyagraha Ashram," reflecting the movement towards passive resistance launched by Gandhi. Gandhi defined an ashram as a "group life in a religious spirit".[12] The word "religious" was used in the widest sense. The individuals living in the ashram did not enforce any ideology or ritual. However, a few rules of personal conduct were advocated, such as certain attributes of universal application. The other rules, such as the eradication of untouchability, physical labour, and the practice of fearlessness, were fostered to mitigate the negativities in Indian society, such as caste-ridden, discounted dignity of labour.

The individuals living in the ashram had to take these vows and observe those vows practically in their lives most intelligently and creatively. These vows were the stepping stones towards moral and spiritual growth. The ashram life was very busy and engaging; everyone was assigned some duty and responsibility. Every person needed to exert some manual work. The ashram had a spinning and weaving department, there was a cowshed and a large farm. The individuals living in the ashram cleaned their plates and washed

---

10 https://madrascourier.com/insight/how-gandhi-built-a-community-began-satyagraha-at-the-sabarmati-ashram/.

11 Gandhi, M.K., *An Autobiography or The Story of My Experiments with Truth*, Ahmedabad: Navajivan, 1948, p. 365.

12 https://www.mkgandhi.org/biography/gndashrm.php.

their clothes. There was no concept of servants in the ashram. The ashram could be visualised as a large family, much like a lot similar to the monastery. It represented a lot like a patriarch, where Gandhi was Bapu, the father of the household, and Kasturba was Ba, the mother. In other words, the ashrams could also be considered a human laboratory where Gandhi tested all his moral and spiritual hypotheses.

The ashram was like a family where members were not connected by blood but by their shared philosophy and fundamental ideologies. Gandhi governed the whole ashram through morality.[13] When anything went wrong or there was a lapse in the system, Gandhi took the blame on himself and felt responsible. The people in the ashram were motivated to foster a new construct of truth and non-violence that helped revolutionize their lifestyle. All activities of independence, coupled with the experiments on the uplift of society, were carried out from Sabarmati Ashram. The purpose of the ashram was twofold: one was to initiate the search for Truth and the other was to create a non-violent group of workers. The non-violent group of workers would become the engine of the freedom movement that would propagate across the whole country.[14]

In Sabarmati Ashram, Gandhi lived in a small cottage known as "Hridaya (Heart) Kunj", a place that holds a historic value. At this place, Gandhi used a writing desk, a khadi kurta, yarn spun by him, and there were letters written by him. Towards the right of his kutir, there was an Ashram guest house, Vinoba Kutir, and Mira Kutir. Another crucial place in the Ashram was Upasana Mandir, an open-air prayer ground, situated between "Hridaya Kunj" and "Magan Kutir". The "Upasana Mandir" was a very crucial place where Gandhi used to address several questions from individuals after the usual prayer. The questions were discussed with utmost care and relevance, and the corresponding solutions were shared.

Everyone seeking to serve society must be motivated to achieve total detachment. On account of the protest against the mill yarn, the members ceased wearing the clothes manufactured by the mill. As khadi became the symbol of national integration and freedom, the ashram adopted khadi as their forefront work. Many women from adjoining areas of the ashram joined as wage labourers in the ashram's khadi production. Many of the women were untouchables, and they were encouraged to join the spinning and weaving work.

---

13 https://www.mkgandhi.org/biography/gndashrm.php.

14 https://www.mkgandhi.org/museum/Sabarmati.php.

In 1930, when Gandhi began his pad yatra or Dandi March from Sabarmati Ashram to Dandi for the Salt Satyagraha, he decided not to return to Sabarmati Ashram until India attained its independence.[15] In 1934, Gandhi selected Wardha for Harijan service and the promotion of village industries. In the Wardha Ashram, fellow inmates were motivated to take up village work, on the same lines as Sabarmati Ashram. Later, Wardha, Central India was decided as the headquarters. Gandhi came to Wardha at the request of Jamnalal Bajaj. Thus, in 1936, Shegaon was established as his residence, later renamed Sevagram, meaning "village of service". Though Jamnalal ji gave his land to the ashram, Gandhi laid a condition that no more than five hundred rupees be spent on the construction of his hut. The uniqueness of the ashram was that it had a common kitchen, and the main purpose of the kitchen was to break the barriers of the caste system. The so-called untouchables were deployed in the common kitchen.

In Sevagram Ashram, Mira Ben began a sanitation programme in Sindi. Gandhi instructed villagers to make earth latrines and explained that the manure produced would not only enhance crop productivity but also enable them to rotate fodder or vegetable crops all year long. Various co-benefits were assured such as improvement in health, elimination of many diseases, and a clean village. In Sindi, people were very protective of their caste interests and were possessive about their culture and festivals.

Sevagram became the epitome of several important matters and movements. It became the central place for several institutions for nation-building activities. The inmates of the ashram lived a very simple life, performing the daily schedule of the ashram that included prayers, spinning, manual labour, cleaning, and farming. The ashram had a bookshop, a dairy farm, and a kitchen that functioned on a biogas plant, also ran a school based on Nai Talim. Thus, Sevagram became a place for national and international pilgrimage, and even now a large number of people visit Sevagram Ashram. Sevagram Ashram achieved remarkable success in implementing a community medical system accessible to all. Sushila and Dr Nayar played an instrumental role in eradicating cholera from Sevagram.[16] The lessons of austerity and abstinence were propagated in the ashram of Sevagram. The experiments in Sevagram laid the foundation for a healthcare system for rural communities and health for all. The community is motivated towards a community-oriented mission, working strongly with alcohol and drug addiction centres.

---

15 https://www.gandhiashramsevagram.org/.

16 https://www.mgims.ac.in/index.php/about-us/history-and-heritage.

The Sevagram or Wardha Ashram was a more peaceful and harmonious community than Sabarmati. In Sevagram, ashram members respected the rules and performed the work assigned sincerely. The members wore products of khadi and clothes woven from yarn spun of excellent quality. The members at Sevagram were small in number, more dedicated, and they were under the guidance and inspiration of Vinobha Bhave. The members were more regulated, disciplined, and consolidated the work more efficiently.

The ashram had various religious men who stayed, such as Tukdoji Maharaj, a saint who sang bhajans, devotional songs. Another resident of the ashram was a Japanese monk, who worked hard morning and evening and, in the evening, could be heard beating his prayer drum and chanting Buddhist mantras.[17] For Gandhi, the Sevagram ashram was a laboratory of ahimsa. What he experimented on there in the ashram could provide him a solution to the larger challenges encountered by the nation. Thus, the ashram was run based on constructive activities related to cleanliness, health, education, agricultural innovation, and self-sufficiency in fuel, energy, water, and food.

However, the ashram faced several shortcomings in the context of disputes and conflicts among themselves, reporting theft. Repeated incidences of illness among the members of the ashram related to malaria, typhoid, fever, and dysentery exacerbated the challenges of running the ashram smoothly. A lot of time and effort were dedicated to the services provided to the sick. Each patient received careful nursing attention.[18] A comprehensive plan of naturopathy and preventive medicine for people was laid down by the members of the ashram. Sevagram ashram was constructed on the lines of a model village. The village lacked hygienic comforts, nutritive food intake, proper sanitation, proper medical aid, and healthcare infrastructure. The experiments related to health care at Sevagram were motivated by the prevention of diseases rather than the cure.

In his ashrams, Gandhi laid down several norms related to hygiene and cleanliness. All the members were trained to live and dwell on the premises of the ashram in a way to demonstrate an ideal lifestyle to villagers. Their living was a noble lesson to villagers at large, or rather a message to the human race. The kitchen, toilets, and premises of the ashram were kept spotless, while the residents cleaned and washed their utensils. Some of the daily activities were compulsory; for example, cleaning the teeth with neem or babul twigs

17 Thomas, Mark, *Gandhi and His Ashrams*, Mumbai, India: Popular Prakashan Pvt. Ltd., 1993, p. 83. https://www.mkgandhi.org/ebks/Gandhi_and_his_Ashrams.pdf.
18 Ibid., 105.

was a compulsory activity.[19] In the beginning, the used twigs were discarded or thrown away; later, Gandhi recommended that these twigs be collected, washed, dried, and then burnt as fuel.

Several day-to-day activities at the ashram life served as lessons in sustainable living for the human race. The peels discarded after cutting vegetables were collected and kept in a compost pit. Further, the waste paper was burnt and converted into manure. The practice of providing separate receptacles for solid and liquid excrement was a remarkable achievement. This activity facilitated the production of manure from solid excrement. Among the specific rules, the residents were instructed to keep themselves away from proper toilets. They were given strong instructions to keep the toilets covered with earth to avoid odour and disease. There were strict instructions for spitting. Thus, from the smallest to the biggest challenges were addressed by Gandhi as a solution through the prescribed living in the ashrams.[20]

The instructive notices were written in a notebook and circulated to the residents by the manager of the ashram. The central focus of the instructions was the emphasis on self-discipline and self-reliance. The activities of the ashram grew naturally according to the changing circumstances, and so did the rules and regulations. Thus, the rules and regulations of the ashram were ever-evolving and progressive. With the onset of endemic diseases like cholera and other illnesses, the need for a proper dispensary was felt in the ashram. Gandhi was against allopathic treatments and dispensaries. However, on the contrary, he was forced to take a course of drugs such as quinine, sodium bicarbonate, potassium permanganate, and iodine. He was curious and troubled about not finding any alternative drugs in the Ayurvedic system.

One of the prominent residents of the ashram, Dr Sushila Nayar, extended medical services to the residents of the ashram and the villagers diligently. Approximately four hundred inoculations were administered, and thus Sevagram survived with only three casualties during the cholera epidemic. Dr Sushila also treated several cases successfully.[21] Soon, an extensive health centre emerged in Sevagram, later developed into a fully equipped hospital, attending extensively to the medical needs of the villagers.[22] Dr Sushila worked with local Harijans who were adequately trained in nursing methods. This is how a robust, successful model was demonstrated at Sevagram as a

19 Ibid., 108.

20 Ibid.

21 Gandhi, M.K., *An Autobiography or The Story of My Experiments with Truth*, Ahmedabad: Navajivan, 1948, p. 330.

22 *Bombay Chronicle*, May 15, 1915.

pilot healthcare model. The medical programme run by Sevagram included an extensive training scheme, motivated to serve the villagers and provide them with relief from disease as much as possible.

Another health issue pointed out by Dr Batra, retired Deputy Director of Public Health from Bengal, was that most of the village children suffered from keratomalacia, a disease caused by a lack of vitamin A. The remedy suggested by Dr Batra was a remarkably successful eradication of the health issue.[23] All village children were gathered in one place and were given six ounces of skim milk with palm gud or syrup and a teaspoon of red palm oil. It was observed that in a few weeks, not a single case of keratomalacia was found in Seagram. Based on this experiment and research-based method, a nationwide campaign was launched against the disease "keratomalacia".[24]

Malaria was the most widespread and serious disease during that time, though its effects were not as devastating as those of cholera and plague. Gandhi deployed the method of research by selecting experts in the field of malaria prevention and launched a nationwide campaign against the disease from the Sevagram Ashram. Some of the preventive efforts involved engineering tasks to deal with mosquito breeding spaces. These efforts included draining the land, filling in pools and ponds, and rectifying water courses.[25] A consistent watch and surveillance of the compound were of utmost necessity to drain the surface water, and kerosene or oil was applied to prevent larvae breeding. Further, sulfur and other repellent substances were burnt in the house to drive out the mosquitoes and insects and make their surroundings mosquito-proof.[26] Also, widespread awareness camps were initiated where the villagers were informed about the larvae in their breeding places.

In addition to these preventive measures, Gandhi promoted dietary reform and played a crucial role in aspects of anti-malaria work. The long-term adoption of a proper diet was instrumental in preventing the malaria epidemic. Therefore, improvement in diet and self-sufficiency in food were identified as integral aspects of village reform. From the prism of agriculture, Gandhi was more concerned about efficient methods of cultivation. He opposed the cultivation of cash crops that raised the revenue of zamindars but rarely benefited the poor tiller or landless labourers. Sevagram became the hub of scientific experiments on agricultural techniques designed to enhance

23 Thomas, Mark, *Gandhi and His Ashrams*, Mumbai, India: Popular Prakashan Pvt. Ltd., 1993, p. 110. https://www.mkgandhi.org/ebks/Gandhi_and_his_Ashrams.pdf.

24 *Bombay Chronicle*, May 15, 1915.

25 Ibid., pp. 331–332.

26 Ibid., p. 333.

quality and crop productivity. The agriculture-related experiments were carried out on land that was brought under cultivation.

The cultivation of crops such as sugarcane and papaya was introduced, which were generally not cultivated in that region. Further, the development of the honey industry at Sevagram was the result of Gandhi's insistence on colonies of bees being set up in the ashram. Thus, Sevagram Ashram immensely enhanced the production of fruits and vegetables.[27] Gandhi wanted to bring a revolution to the dietary habits of people through his innovative experiments in agricultural practices. However, villagers failed to acknowledge the significance of the food they consumed and its relationship with their health and well-being. Gandhi advocated that only those fruits and vegetables grown on the ashram premises should be consumed and used in the kitchen. Moreover, he insisted that food be eaten raw to conserve fuel. The ashram faced a shortage of vegetables due to insufficient production. Though Gandhi promoted a life of simplicity, it did not mean that an individual must consume only the same food all the time; he believed in variety and insisted on growing a variety of fruits and vegetables in the ashram.

Another experiment done in Sevagram was the palm jaggery industry developed by Sevagram. The experiment started with 25 trees; later, this cultivation or industry developed on a cooperative basis. However, this industry faced a challenge due to its involvement in making "nira" syrup, which was opposed by the Parsi community.[28] Among the other agricultural experiments at Sevagram, animal husbandry was the most efficient industry. Several scientific experiments and research were initiated by Balwant Singh, who later became an expert in "goseva", cow service. An elaborate study was conducted on cow milk and its uses. Various activities were initiated for cow protection, including extensive activities such as cattle breeding and cooperative milk distribution. The cattle-breeding and farming departments of the ashram were separated from the milk department. The ultimate aim of Gandhi was to establish a cooperative dairy in the village.

The ashram began to provide mass employment to various sections of society, even in the surrounding villages. Various cooperative organizations emerged, such as "Charkha Parishramalaya", (spinning wheel work centre), established to popularise khadi in the village. Another initiative, known as "Charkha Sangh", (Spinning Wheel Association), was an initiative to safeguard against unemployment and underemployment. The main

27 Tendulkar, D.G., et al., eds., *Gandhiji. His Life and Work,* Bombay: Keshav Bhikaji Dhawale, 1944.

28 Gandhi to Maganlal Gandhi, January 20, 1918, pp. 160–161.

task of individuals associated with these initiatives was to promote handmade products in place of factory products. For instance, khadi in place of mill cloth, village earthen pots instead of factory-made china, reed pens instead of steel pens, handmade paper instead of ordinary paper, babul twigs instead of toothbrushes, ordinary village jaggery instead of factory sugar, and hand-pounded whole rice instead of mill-polished rice. According to Gandhi, the economic uplift of a village could be visualised by opening avenues that would benefit all individuals in the society. For Gandhi, the economic benefit must be associated with moral and social uplift, as, according to him, only material growth or uplift can never be sustainable and would never address the goal of sustainability.

Another initiative, "Hindustani Talimi Sangh" (All India Board of Education) was launched at Sevagram. The education system developed at Sevagram by Gandhi was referred to as "Basic Education", or "Nai Talim".[29] This was an initiative for restructuring the Indian education pattern. Education constitutes the basis of society and is an integral factor for building social, political, and economic reforms. In this context, "nai talim" was introduced in 1937, marking the beginning of Gandhi's most crucial experiment in constructive work. He believed in the principle of free and compulsory education. Gandhi insisted on vocational education, utilising mental, physical, and spiritual potentialities. According to the new framework of the education system, education was imparted through handicraft training or adopting a specific handicraft skill. The main motive behind acquiring handicraft skills was to inculcate the spirit of lifelong learning.

Gandhi promoted manual work not for recreation, passion, or pursuit of knowledge but recommended activities that would be instrumental in the overall development of the individual as a member of a cooperative and democratic community.[30] The elementary thought behind "Basic education", was that each child is made to perform manual labour and productive work, and the training to be given by the school.[31] The medium of instruction should be the mother tongue, and free education is to be provided for seven years on the national level.[32]Such a system of education was gradually expected to cover all the expenses or remuneration of the teachers.[33]

29 Balwantsinha (Balwant Singh), *Under the Shelter of Bapu*, translated from the original in Hindi, Ahmedabad: Navajivan, 1962, p. 150.
30 *Young India*, November 20, 1924.
31 *Indian Annual Register*, 1935, Vol. I, p. 79.
32 *Harijan*, August 24, 1935.
33 Ibid.

Joseph Jean Lanza del Vasto, an Italian aristocrat, deeply influenced by Gandhian thoughts, travelled to India to meet Gandhi to learn the lessons to uproot violence. Gandhi gave another name to Lanza "Shantidas", meaning "Servant of Peace". In 1948, Lanza founded the first Community of Ark to remember Gandhi. Based on the principles of "bread labor", advocated by Gandhi and Tolstoy, everyone in the Community of Ark was required to produce life's basic needs such as food and clothing.[34] The system of bread labour avoided the kind of oppression that occurs when certain sections of society try to avoid work. This practice also avoided division into classes of workers and non-workers. Such a community based on bread labour depicted a "nonviolent economy" that abuses neither people nor nature.

The residents of the Community of Ark produced everything they used in their daily lives. Their purpose was to break any connection with the modern economy, largely because modern society was constituted of injustice towards the poor. The community used simple tools, powered by hand or animal, since all complicated machinery was a product of greed. The simple tools were associated with building mental, physical, and spiritual health. The community grew vegetables and grains using horses and hand methods, while dairy provided milk and cheese. Killing animals for food was avoided; the women spun wool and wove clothes for garments. Other practices included carpentry, fine woodworking, stonecutting, pottery, and printing.

The energy system in the community was self-sufficient; firewood cut from the community's forests was used for indoor heating, water heating, and cooking. Candles were used for indoor lighting. There existed a water-powered sawmill to generate electricity. Each person in the community worked according to ability and received according to need. The individuals did not own money, or any property, or possess personal items such as clothes and books. Each person was allowed to follow their belief system and religion. They believed that peace among people could be visualized only when individuals gained inner peace. Though the people of the Community of Ark attempted to demonstrate a peaceful, non-violent, self-reliant, and self-sustaining society to the Western world, we witness greed, ignorance, violence, and technology that magnifies the negative impact of a violent world.

---

34 https://www.satyagrahafoundation.org/island-of-peace-lanza-del-vasto-and-the-community-of-the-ark/.

The experiments of Gandhi through his ashrams have been recognised in India and abroad, in political and non-political development processes. However, one cannot say India explored the capitalistic growth of humans and still falls back on the ashrams of Gandhi on and off in search of solutions to global challenges of climate change, energy transition, sustainable development goals, and so on.

Chapter 6

SUSTAINABLE PRACTICES BY TRIBAL VILLAGES IN INDIA

With the advent of climate change, ecological crises and concerns demand sustainable practices in life. On one side, India is moving aggressively on the path of economic development and growth, and on the other side, India has to strike the ecological balance of sustainable growth and living. The trade-off between the two is plausible by identifying sustainable practices in life that minimise environmental and ecological degradation. The ashrams of Gandhi depicted the most sustainable practices as described in Chapter 5. India is home to a large number of people belonging to various racial groups, ethnic groups, cultural backgrounds, and social structures. Among the diverse groups of people, a large section of India lives close to nature. The tribal societies belonging to remote areas represent an ethnic base of Indigenous communities with their unique pattern of living, originating from nature.

With the advent of global concerns about environmental sustainability, the United Nations Conference on Environment and Development (UNCED) was held in Rio in June 1992. It was stated that "human beings are the center of concerns for sustainable development and indigenous communities have a vital role in environmental management and development because of their ecologically sustainable knowledge and approaches towards the environment" (Singh and Khare, 1993).[1] This declaration gave a strong message to the world to recognise the role of traditional knowledge systems of indigenous communities and encouraged their active participation in the pathways of achieving sustainable development goals.

1 Singh, S., Khare, A., "People's Participation in Forest Management," *The Commonwealth Forestry Review*, 1993, 72(4), pp. 279–283.

Approximately 8.2 per cent of the total population are tribals of India, consisting of 461 tribal communities.[2] The tribal communities face certain socioeconomic issues such as poverty, illiteracy, diseases, and unemployment. India consists of a large number of primitive tribes who sustain themselves through hunting, fishing, or simple forms of agricultural practices. Such tribes are called "aboriginal tribes". These are considered the oldest ethnological sectors. There may be cultural differences related to lifestyle and traditional practices across various tribes belonging to different parts of the country. However, there is a basic unity in the philosophical orientation among the people born and brought up in an environment close to nature and also in an environment of diversity across nations. Over the years, due to the unprecedented use of natural resources and the need to conserve natural resources, the forest tribes are gradually fading away. Due to excessive droughts or famines, floods, and other natural calamities and the devastating effects of climate change, most of the forests are dying out. Consequently, these tribes are compelled to leave their traditional practices, and the elementary traditional knowledge of indigenous sustainable practices is slowly fading away.

It is crucial to comprehend that indigenous knowledge based on ecological understanding is essential not only for meeting the daily needs of tribal communities but also contributes immensely to the social, cultural, economic, and religious institutions of that region. The interconnectedness with nature exhibited by the tribal groups, small farmers, marginalised populations, and so on, makes them more vulnerable to environmental crises and the risk of losing their traditional knowledge (Denton, 2002; Ramdas, 2009; Sati & Juyal, 2008; Clay, 2003). [3456]Thus, learning from such tribal communities and including the best practices of these communities in policy formulations will help achieve the Sustainable Development Goal 8 (SDG 8), which promotes sustained, inclusive, and sustainable economic growth, full and productive employment, and decent work.

2 https://www.tribesindia.com/tribal-people-in-india/#:~:text=The%20tribes%20of%20India%20constitute,were%20identify%20as%20sub%2Dgroups.

3 Denton, F., "Climate Change Vulnerability, Impacts, and Adaptations: Why does Gender Matter?" *Gender and Development*, 2002, 10(2), pp. 10–20.

4 Ramdas, S.R., "Women, Forest Space and the Law: Transgressing the Boundaries," *Economic and Political Weekly*, 2009, 44(44), pp. 65–73.

5 Sati, M.C., Juyal, R.P., "A Gender Approach to Sustainable Rural Development of Mountains: Women's Successes in Agro-enterprises in the Indian Central Himalayan Region,". *Mountain Research and Development*, 2008, 28(1), pp. 8–12.

6 Clay, R., "Speaking Up: Women's Voices in Environmental Decision Making," *Environmental Health Perspectives*, 2003, 111(1), pp. A34–A37.

Apart from addressing environmental issues, tribal and Indigenous societies can address climate change and disaster-related challenges. The close association and dependency of Indigenous, rural populations on the natural ecosystem will help identify any changes in the climate as well as deliver practical Indigenous solutions or adaptive measures.[7] Various mitigation and adaptive activities and measures will find several feasible, cost-effective, participatory, and sustainable outcomes. The tribal communities have a profound social element that enhances social-ecological systems and social cohesion within communities (Berkes et al., 2003).[8] It is observed that resilient social-ecological systems are more efficient in adapting to changes in climate and tackling associated ecosystem services (Blondel, 2006).[9]

The Indigenous knowledge of tribal communities and their best practices to live in harmony with nature have enabled them to predict nature and disasters related to nature to a very large extent. People in tribal communities could predict monsoons and inform about the cultivation or agriculture yield in advance. They were able to predict the probability of occurrence of drought or flood calamities. Some ancient Hindu sutras predict monsoons and inform people about the potential yield of agriculture.[10] Several indicators are taken into account while predicting nature, such as the colour and the direction of flow of clouds, and lightning in the clouds. For instance, if the clouds are rough and small, tossed about by the wind, and have the shape of a camel, corms, dead bodies, monkeys, or other inauspicious creatures, then the region will neither have prosperity nor rain in the land. Further, Indigenous people living in Rajasthan are vulnerable to drought, floods, famines, food security, and so on. To encounter these vulnerabilities, local tribal communities developed a variety of measures such as growing drought-resistant and early-maturing indigenous crop varieties, gathering a variety of fruits and vegetables, wetlands cultivation, livestock, and diversification, enabling the communities to survive climate hazards. Thus, their knowledge

7 Mukhopadhyay, R., Roy, S.B., "Traditional Knowledge for Biodiversity Conservation, Maintain Ecosystem Services and Livelihood Security in the Context of Climate Change: Case Studies from West Bengal, India," *Journal of Biodiversity*, 2015, 6(1–2), pp. 22–29.

8 Berkes, F., Colding, J., Folke, C., "Navigating Social Ecological Systems: Building Resilience for Complexity and Change," *Ecology and Society*, 2003, 9(1), p. 1.

9 Blondel, J., "The Design of Mediterranean Landscapes: A Millennial Story of Humans and Ecological Systems during the Historic Period," *Human Ecology*, 2006, 34, pp. 713–729.

10 Pareek, A., Trivedi, P.C., *Cultural Values and Indigenous Knowledge of Climate Change and Disaster Prediction in Rajasthan*, India, 2011.

and preparedness, administrative structures, and social institutions helped cope with disaster-related hazards.

Medicinal plants and livelihood are other aspects significantly addressed by the traditional knowledge system of tribal, rural, and remote areas. Medicinal plants constitute a livelihood option and a significant driver for biodiversity conservation. Equitable access and benefit-sharing arrangements for locally available biodiversity resources were promoted by The Biological Diversity Act 2002.[11] Moreover, there is an urgent need to develop the adaptive capacity of people to maintain soil health and nutrition conditions for crop protection. In the present era, there is a rising disconnect between agro-ecosystems and ecological processes, owing to the excessive use of chemicals and fertilizers, and so on.[12] Thus, reviving the traditional system of organic farming and other agronomic practices will balance the use of chemicals and can offer sustainable, productive solutions.[13] Thus, the tribal communities demonstrate and depict the most robust pathways to accomplishing Sustainable Development Goal 13 (SDG 13), which involves taking urgent actions to combat climate change.

In post-independence India, the tribal communities are constantly struggling to retain access to their ancestral land. The Forest Conservation Amendment Bill, passed in the Lok Sabha on July 26, 2023, redefines the legal definition of "forest", narrowing down the scope, and potentially excluding areas even if they hold ecological and environmental significance. Most of the tribal regions in India are sacred sites and act as repositories of spiritual and ecological significance. Most of them are located in ecologically rich areas, representing hubs of biodiversity. The tribal communities inherently maintain ecological balance and mitigate climate change. Their rituals and traditions are systematically linked to promote the sustainable use of natural resources. For example, practices such as tree worship, water conservation rituals, and bans on hunting certain species contribute immensely to the preservation of natural resources. Moreover, one can find several sacred groves across India such as Devrai (Maharashtra), Orans (Rajasthan), Sama (Bihar), Devban (Himachal Pradesh), and kavu (Kerela) are instrumental in maintaining the ecosystem intact for carbon sequestration, nutrient recycling,

11 https://www.indiacode.nic.in/bitstream/123456789/2046/4/a2003-18.pdf.

12 Mukhopadhyay, R., Roy, S.B., "Traditional Knowledge for Biodiversity Conservation, Maintain Ecosystem Services and Livelihood Security in the Context of Climate Change: Case Studies from West Bengal, India," *Journal of Biodiversity*, 2015, 6(1–2), pp. 22–29.

13 Ibid.

topsoil preservation, and biodiversity conservation that are essential for climate resilience.

In the mid-1990s, a devotional tradition called the Sarna movement emerged among Jharkhand women centred around sacred groves with Sal trees. The ritual involved the presence of mystic experiences around the sacred grove. Thus, the preservation of these sacred sites fosters a sense of community cohesion. The communities came together to protect these areas, promoting collective action towards environmental conservation and resilience against climate change impacts. Dewulf et al. (2005) and Smith and Sharp (2012) asserted that Indigenous communities possess invaluable, context-specific knowledge and resources. Integrating the knowledge of resources and sustainable practices of these Indigenous communities can significantly provide feasible and sustainable solutions to mitigate climate change impacts.

The tribal communities of the Pachmarhi[14] biosphere grew plant species in their agricultural land and home gardens. The most prominent tribal communities in that region are Gond and Korku. The community grows and adopts two types of cropping patterns, rabi and kharif. The agricultural activities are accomplished with certain specific cultural practices, followed by vibrant ceremonies before and after the harvesting of crops. Initially, they dig a hole in a corner of the agricultural land where they sow some traditional varieties of cultivated crops, followed by offering a coconut and a cup of "mahua liquor" to a local deity named "Sayenibuda". This practice is performed only once a year, and once the crop is ready to harvest, the head of the household offers some milk and mahua liquor to the deity in the crop field, and thereafter, harvesting of the crop is allowed. Other methods, such as bio-fencing are used by erecting the branches of some plants such as "nirgundi" around the boundary of the crop fields along with the usual rituals they perform to protect the crop. They fix a branch of "semacarpus" on the lunar eclipse with the faith that this will reduce the insects.[15] They spray ashes of wood around the crop field to keep the pests or insects away. According to one of the rituals, referred to as "Ujagar", a handful of unboiled rice is picked up and each person offers it to the village diety along with the village priest.

Around forty-seven varieties of species are grown in the region. These species are known for their significance as food, medicine, vegetables, fodder,

14 Kala, C.P., "Traditional Ecological Knowledge of Tribal Communities and Sustainability of Nature and Natural Resources in Pachmarhi Biosphere Reserve in India," *International Journal of Ecology*, 2022, 2022(1), p. 5979024.

15 Kala, C P., "Traditional Farming System of Gond and Other Communities in the Pachmarhi Biosphere Reserve of India," *Applied Ecology and Environmental Sciences*, 2015, 3(5), pp. 140–145.

and nutraceuticals. These traditional religious practices are extremely ecologically sustainable. However, it has been witnessed that with the invention of hybrid seeds, the traditional practice of growing indigenous crops has significantly declined over the years. These tribal communities are also well aware of the soil types based on soil texture, amounting to almost sixteen soil types. Soil moisture is a crucial parameter to indicate the fertility of the soil.[16] The tribal community believes that the groundwater is purer than other sources.

Natural resources such as rivers, water, forests, birds, animals, and hills are inseparable from the lives of tribals as their day-to-day life revolves around these bounties of nature. Though the tribal people do not believe in saving natural resources for the future, they refrain from overexploitation of natural resources. They do not remove trees while practising agriculture because they are well aware of their significance in providing organic matter to the soil and helping in preventing soil erosion. The tribal people maintain their home gardens where they grow necessary vegetables to meet their day-to-day requirements of food and dietary diversity.

The home gardens play an instrumental role in enriching the social life of the tribal community. The people exchange a variety of fruits and vegetables and cook together on occasion. The home gardens also become a major source of preserving some medicinal plants and vegetables holding great nutritive value. Thus, the tribal lifestyle based on traditional indigenous practices becomes a driving source for preserving the rare species of plants and vegetables. They have deep knowledge of the conservation of soil fertility by adopting various traditional practices such as crop rotation, burning crop residue, applying manure, and planting tree species. A symbiosis between traditional ecological knowledge, traditional and religious practices, and the belief system together develops a robust and resilient system for climate change, disaster, and ecological sustainability. This knowledge is systematically passed on from one generation to another. Thus, nature and natural ecosystems are naturally ingrained within the tribal community and they are not separate entities for which they have to worry about.

The remarkable symbiosis between traditional ecological knowledge, traditional and religious practices, and the belief system is an outcome of the philosophical evolution of tribal communities. The tribals believe in the

16 Kala, C.P., "Traditional Ecological Knowledge on Characteristics, Conservation and Management of Soil in Tribal Communities of Pachmarhi Biosphere Reserve, India," *Journal of Soil Science and Plant Nutrition,* 2013, 13(1), pp. 201–214. https://doi.org/10.4067/s0718-95162013005000018.

fundamental principle of kinship (Mandelbaum, 1970).[17] Equality remains their basic organising principle. However, some of the tribal communities are highly individualistic and do not depend on others in any sense. They do incorporate new groups or members into their tribe but in the form of fictive kinsmen. The tribals usually believe that life being uncertain so they do not seek long-term rewards. They usually seek pleasure and value leisure more than work. They believe in acquiring pleasure and wealth and are willing to work against the values and opinions of society. The tribals combine the short-term benefits of religion and its long-term transcendental function.

The underlying ideological framework of tribals comprises various layers of relationships (Surajit Sinha, 1957).[18] One is the man-to-supernatural relationship, the second is the man–nature relationship, and finally the third one is the man-to-man relationship. Rituals in the community are mainly to avoid sickness and death. There is no specific belief system regarding heaven or hell; however, faith in magic remains popular. In the man–nature relationship sphere, the natural universe is constantly a part of the relationship between man and nature. Under the man-to-man relationships, the relationships are confined to their tribal world. All human beings are believed to be active and do not seek any stratification. The people in the community consider all people as equal. The elders are respected, children are valued, and barrenness is feared. The communities dominate social life, they emphasise pleasure and believe in reciprocal and obligatory relationships. They discard celibacy and asceticism and believe in enjoying life and other material pleasures.

Another tribal ethnic base of India is the indigenous group of people who took shelter in the depths of mountains. These aboriginal tribes are further divided and subdivided into a large number of sub-tribes. All of these sub-tribes are mutually exclusive, having an identity of their own culture, customs, traditional practices, and lifestyle. However, they all have certain common features, such as they live away from the civilised world in an inaccessible part of forests and hills. They have a unique dialect of their own, maintaining their primitive occupation. They have nomadic habits and live naked or semi-naked. The overall life of the tribal people is a simple and placid but tough life. They have a rich cultural legacy comprising myths and

17 Mandelbaum, D.G., *Society in India: Continuity and Change,* Vol. 1, Berkeley: University of California Press, 1978.

18 Sinha, S., "Tribal Cultures of Peninsular India as a Dimension of Little Tradition in the Study of Indian Civilisation: A Preliminary Statement," *The Journal of American Folklore,* 1958, 71(281), pp. 504–518.

legends that are interesting but rather strange. These indigenous traditional tribes are emotionally connected with their ecological surroundings. Their mythological tales reflect a substantial aspect of their life.

The Muria is a tribe belonging to Madhya Pradesh that has "The ghotul", a village dormitory, which is a central institution and a highly democratic organization. It is a kind of school that provides co-education in every sphere of tribal life. These communities have witnessed a gradual social change, which is not simply a mechanical change of addition and subtraction but is the integration of new systems among the old ones. Thus, social evolution involves diffusion, implying the spread of knowledge and customs from one set of people to another. Moreover, the customs that regulate the ownership or transfer of land among the primitive tribes are significantly different from those in modern societies. Transforming the trusteeship of tribal land to absolute ownership of land has been widely witnessed in recent times.

Another prominent tribal region is the Kinnaur district of Himachal Pradesh, reflecting old legendary and mythological land. Being located at an elevation, the region has a temperate climate with long winters. Consequently, avalanches occur during the winter season. The region lies in a seismic focus and suffers from tremors of varying intensity and earthquakes. One of the most devastating earthquakes occurred was in 1975. The area is abundant in natural resources, and the water supply is mainly dependent on the melting of snow. The water from springs is used for drinking and washing clothes. The region coincidentally faces severe poverty due to the low productivity of agriculture and the absence of occupations. There exists a huge potential for subsidiary occupations, including activities such as dairying, sheep and goat rearing, and poultry.

The tribal communities in this region have inherently adopted traditional methods of conserving social, cultural, and biological resources. They have designed effective devices and strategies for the conservation of natural resources.[19] The tribals have developed a symbiotic relationship between endowed biological resources and cultural diversities. The tribals even used scientific methods to upgrade the old systems for better hydropower use, such as irrigation of crops, water for drinking, and so on. Nutritive crops like barley and buckwheat were cultivated, and approximately twenty crops were cultivated as staple food. The rotation of farm fields allowed for the replenishment of nutrients. Approximately fifteen plant species were found to

19 Lal, C., Prasher, R.S., "Traditional Knowledge Systems and Conservation Practices in Tribal Society of Western Himalayas: A Case Study of District Kinnaur of Himachal Pradesh," *International Journal of Farm Sciences*, 2016, 6(3), pp. 159–171.

be used by local people for medicinal purposes to foster a healthcare system. Finally, it is observed that the tribal people of Kinnaur district in Himachal Pradesh have indigenous conservation techniques conserving age-old traditions, culture, and natural resources. The tribal population is well aware of the significance of environmental protection. Their sociocultural diversity and environmental complexity have significantly favoured tribal people in developing a symbiotic relationship with locally available resources and the precarious nature. Such environmentally conducive practices have helped the people in the better pursuit of livelihood.

Further, several tribes from Tripura have demonstrated different modes of sustainable living. The tribals of Tripura used blocks of charcoal, broken down into powder form and mixed with water, to make a paste used for cleaning the teeth.[20] A product known as loofah gently exfoliates the skin without scratching or causing irritation to remove dead skin, is made using biodegradable and environmentally friendly methods by the tribals in Tripura. Moreover, the tribals from Tripura traditionally derived shampoo from charcoal and ash residues. The liquid extracted after filtering out charcoal bits and ashes, called "chakhwi", is used to prepare a traditional dish of Tripura. The filtered chakhwi is collected in a bowl, which is later used as a shampoo.

The traditional houses of tribes of Tripura are made of bamboo, a widely available raw material in Tripura. The houses made of bamboo are called "Gairing", small huts with a raised platform and bamboo stairs, surrounded by an open balcony. However, with extensive modernisation, people began to move to cities and abandoned living in huts. Another biodegradable product made by tribes is a hand fan made of palm leaves. The hand fan is made of leaves of wine palm, which are dried and cut down to make beautiful hand fans. Thus, the tribal people make the most readily available products from nature. They grow their food on their own or collect food from nature; the day-to-day products used by them are made from nature. With the advent of climate change, it is crucial to recognise the contribution of the tribal people in conserving natural resources.

The loss of biodiversity on account of excessive consumption and production processes of humankind is the most alarming challenge in the present era. The role of tribals in preserving biodiversity is of great significance. Their traditional knowledge of preserving useful species of medicinal plants and vegetables is the most sustainable solution in the present times. The best practices adopted by tribals, coupled with their knowledge and skills, would

20 https://www.adivasilivesmatter.com/post/5-sustainable-lifestyle-practices-of-tribes-from-tripura.

strengthen the sustainable pathways to achieve Sustainable Development Goal 12 (SDG 12), which is production of goods and services that improve the quality of life. Various awareness programmes can be organized in collaboration with the tribal communities to save and conserve the most useful medicinal plants, which are extremely necessary for health and well-being. Such initiatives will help achieve the Sustainable Development Goal 15 (SDG 15). When people are aware of the nutritive and medicinal content of plant species and trees around them, they will certainly make conscious efforts to replant and preserve them.

In addition to sustainable practices demonstrated by the tribal communities, these communities reflect the most robust decision-making system. In any society or community, the backbone of socio-cultural and traditional ethos is its political and governance system. For a peaceful, self-sufficient, and self-reliant community, the system of governance has to be stable and resilient. Most of the tribal communities adopt a consensus-based, participatory model of governance where each member of the community has the complete right or voice in the decision-making of the community.

Another village, Mendha, is a small village of Gonda tribals in central India, in the Dhanora tehsil of Gadchiroli district in the State of Maharashtra. Some of the unique characteristics of this tribal community are the non-existence of disputes and differences of opinion in the village, no problem of poverty, hunger, or unemployment, and no economic disparities. The village functions on a consensus-based decision-making system to make critical decisions of the village community under a village assembly called *the gaon-samaj-sabha,* comprising all the adult villagers as its members. In one of the meetings of the village assembly, it was decided to impose a fine of Rs.150 on the practice of cutting trees in the forest for fruits, leaves, branches, or even honey. Even though the villagers are highly dependent on forests for food and fuel and use biogas as a source of energy, they all respected the decision of the assembly and complied with the decision unanimously.[21]

Thus, the consensus-based, decentralised decision-making system adopted by the tribal communities is the most sustainable and peaceful system. It is devoid of the accumulation of wealth, mass consumption, and private ownership and follows the trusteeship model. It ultimately generates a more peaceful, non-violent economy. This system makes the tribal people realise their social and political responsibility, making each person responsible and liable for every act of production and consumption. Thus, the Sustainable

21 Tofa, D.N., Hiralal, M.H. Mendha (Lekha), *The Village that Declared that 'We Have Our Government in Delhi and Mumbai, But in Our Village We Ourselves are the Government.'*"

Development Goal (SDG) 12, which ensures sustainable consumption and production patterns, can be visualized by the consensus-based, decentralised governance system.

In any community, the decision is crucial and should reflect the best interests of the community and not individual vested interests.[22] Colonisation has significantly affected the decision-making processes in indigenous communities. Individualised thoughts conflict with communal ideals. Consensus decision-making is an alternative to the "top-down" decision-making process adopted by hierarchical groups. When leaders or hierarchical groups make decisions in a way that does not include the participation of all interested stakeholders, the decisions do not represent the interests of all the members or the full agreement of the community. This system is referred to as a "top-down" approach.

All tribal communities have strong social control and a unique traditional system, possessing a rich cultural heritage.[23] These indigenous communities have maintained their cultural identities. Consequently, the customary laws are based on their belief system, values, traditions, perceptions, and mythologies that propagate their social and cultural heritage. The customary codes or social codes are essential conditions for the solidarity and prosperity of the community. Therefore, in the absence of these customary codes, there would be utter chaos in the community. Studies suggest that tribal communities still regulate and support their systems with their local institutions that control the lives of people in the community (Rao, 2000; Singh, 2000).[24][25] The tribal self-governance institutions and traditional village panchayat, also called "Kula panchayat", perform several responsibilities of safeguarding and promoting the economic interests of the villagers, celebrating religious rites and festivals, protecting cultural heritage, and maintaining the continuity of folk dances, traditional skills, knowledge, and so on. Thus, self-governance institutions hold a crucial place in village governance despite the presence of Panchayats.

---

22 Horn-Miller, K., "What does Indigenous Participatory Democracy Look Like: Kahnawake's Community Decision Making Process," *Review of Constitutional Studies*, 2013, 18, p. 111.

23 Rao, N.S., "Interface of Tribal Self-Governance Institutions and Statutory Panchayats: A Study in the Scheduled Areas of Andhra Pradesh," *National Institute of Rural Development & Panchayati Raj. Hyderabad: Centre for Development Documentation and Communication NIRDPR*, 2017.

24 Singh, K.S., "Tribal Customary Laws: Policy Implications," *Yojana*, April 2000.

25 Mohan Rao, K., "Traditional Tribal Panchayats," *Yojana*, April 2000. Mukul, "Tribal Areas: Transition to Self-Governance," *Economic and Political Weekly*, 1997, 32(18), pp. 928–929.

Consequently, maintaining a harmonious balance between their lifestyle and ecology, the tribal communities reflect a remarkable symbiosis of socio-ecological traditions that constitute a fundamental aspect of sustainability. Thus, the tribals are the "Real Heroes" of India, the warriors and custodians of our nature. Apart from environmentally sustainable practices, the tribals demonstrate disaster-resilient practices that survive the greatest disasters, providing adequate preparedness. Several agricultural practices adopted by tribes are highly productive. In addition, biodiversity conservation, preserving medicinal plants, and so on, are some of the most relevant and crucial methods that can be adopted by tribal communities. The consumption and production processes and lifestyle of these communities are substantially ecologically sustainable. Finally, the consensus-based decision-making system deployed by the tribals delivers a very peaceful, non-violent, and self-sufficient community.

CONCLUSION: NON-VIOLENCE AND THE ECOLOGICAL IMPERATIVE

Today, we face the prospect of a nature endangered on a global scale, and along with it, a big threat to our moral structures. The urgent crisis menacing humanity today is the possibility of systemic ecological catastrophe, and the most tragic dimension of this threat is mankind's indifference to its own mistakes. Immanuel Kant famously argued that the human race progresses towards moral perfection. As he argued: "I will thus be allowed to assume that, since the human race is constantly advancing concerning culture as the natural end for the same, it is also progressing toward the better concerning the moral end of its existence, and that this progress will occasionally be *interrupted* but never *broken off*. It is not necessary for me to prove this supposition, rather my opponent has the burden of proof."[1] The destruction of Nature by Man, however, questions the limits of Kant's ethical theory and its normative guidance for dealing with the challenges of climate change. If we agree that climate change is caused by the nature of our *modus vivendi*, we can agree with Alice Pinheiro Walla that

> the greatest limitation of Kant's ethical theory in regard to climate ethics is that it is *anthropocentric*. It is based on respect for rational nature in our person and in the person of others and therefore excludes the possibility of direct obligations towards the environment. However, Kant's ethical theory does not leave us with a deontological "vacuum" in regard to the environment. He accounts for duties towards non-human animals and nature in general as indirect duties to oneself. Cruelty to animals and wanton destruction of nature not only have a bad influence on one's moral character but they also reveal an immoral disposition. Insensitivity to beauty in nature and to the destruction of

1 Kant, Immanuel, "On the Common Saying: This May be True in Theory, but It Does Not Hold in Practice," in *Toward Perpetual Peace and Other Writings on Politics, Peace, and History*, New Haven: Yale University Press, 2008, p. 62.

> the environment reveals something very deep about oneself. A person who is cruel to animals is hardened against suffering in general.[2]

Suffering for the planet Earth is the basic principle of considering oneself as a living being. In other words, humans should be presented as living beings among others. From this angle, there is no such thing as a private use of the planet Earth. Mankind privatised the Earth and created the concept of private property. John Locke argued in the *Second Treatise of Government* that, although God gave the Earth to mankind to share in common, it was permissible to enclose parcels of it for private use, so long as there would be enough left over for everyone. Consequently, no space was left for plants and animals, and even the oceans and the mountains were colonised by the modern free will of mankind. As a result, the whole conception of "life" and "living" was distorted and changed.

The concept of "life" comes from the ancient Greek word "*bios*". The ancient Greeks had two words to express life. On the one hand, they used the word "*bios*" and on the other, they referred to the concept of "*zoe*". *Zoe* represented life in general, and *bios* characterised a specific life. In short, *zoe* meant the big picture of life, and *bios* referred to the details of life. Human beings tend to look towards both *zoe* and *bios*. We all look at life, either in a close-up or in a long shot. Actually, there are very few individuals who can see the big picture of life while also examining all its details. Mahatma Gandhi was among the rare human beings who could see the bigger picture of life while approaching life in its details. Unlike the broken and distorted image that we have of life in a consumer society, Gandhi believed in what he called the "Law of Life". He argued: "I have found that life persists in the midst of destruction and therefore there must be a higher law than that of destruction. Only under that law would a well-ordered society be intelligible and life worth living. And if that is the law of life, we have to work it out in daily life."[3] In other words, for Gandhi, life is a perpetual triumph over death. But life is not only about the living and dying of human beings, though we are the ones who give a spiritual and philosophical meaning to life and death. In Gandhi's opinion, life is the total sum of the energy of all living beings. That is why Gandhi says that all life is one. If that is the case, then animals and plants, as much as mountains and oceans, have a kinship with us. Therefore,

---

2 Walla, Alice Pinheiro, "Kant and Climate Change: A Territorial Rights Approach," in *Moral Theory and Climate Change*, Vol. 1, edited by Dale E. Miller, Ben Eggleston, London: Routledge, 2020, p. 104.

3 Gandhi, Mohandas K., *All Men are Brothers*, edited by Krishna Kripalani, Ahmedabad: Navajivan Publishing House, 1971, p. 140.

recognising and respecting *the otherness of the Other* (the Other being anyone or anything which lives) is the foundation of green non-violence.

But the question which comes to mind immediately is: How does Mahatma Gandhi develop this idea of *the otherness of the Other* as the heart of his concept of life? The answer is in *Young India* (July 8, 1926). He explains: "My ethics not only permit me to claim but requires me to own kinship with not merely the ape but the horse and the sheep, the lion and the leopard, the snake and the scorpion."[4] Gandhi's basic assumption here is that one should respect life by being a friend and protector of Nature. As such, Gandhi argues: "Man through the cow is enjoined to realize his identity with all that lives [...] the cow is poem of pity. One reads pity in the gentle animal. She is the mother to millions of Indian mankind."[5] And the cow seems to talk back to humans and say, as Gandhi underlines it: "You are not appointed over us to kill us and eat our flesh or otherwise ill-treat us, but to be our friend and guardian."[6]

Reading these passages by Gandhi, we can deduce that his priority has been Life in general, and not only human life. That is how Gandhi is showing us the way of integral ecology. He sees life in its larger dimension and his non-violence is essentially green and with ecological imperatives. As Thomas Vettickal puts it: "Gandhi's conception of what might now be called a spirituality of ecology was based on a holistic perspective derived from Indian culture, which does offer a holistic perspective to ecology [...]. This new sense of the sacredness of the earth and of our communion with the whole natural environment would lead to another kind of development, i.e., sustainable development, and another kind of technology, i.e., appropriate technology [...]. Gandhi's insights on ecological ways of living, appropriate technology, people centred developments, and village-oriented economy stand out as realizable alternative visions of tomorrow."[7]

Gandhi writes: "I do not want to live at the cost of the life even of a snake. I should let him bite me to death rather than kill him."[8] Some might think that by saying this Gandhi appears as a backward traditionalist who does not understand the advantages of techno-scientific progress. However, what some scientists and technocrats miss enormously is that Mahatma Gandhi is very

4 Quoted in Vettickal, Thomas, *Sarvodaya of Mahatma Gandhi: Realistic Utopia*, (Thesis) University of Toronto, 1998, p. 328.

5 Ibid.

6 Gandhi, Mohandas K., *Truth is God*, Ahmedabad: Navajivan Publishing House, 1959, p. 105.

7 Quoted in Vettickal, Thomas, *Sarvodaya of Mahatma Gandhi: Realistic Utopia*, (Thesis) University of Toronto, 1998, pp. 330, 331, 333.

8 Quoted in *Young India*, April 14, 1927.

well conscious of the power of modernity. In addition to this, he is also trying to elaborate a philosophy of life against the illimitable and uncontrolled power of modern technology. This is how he is proceeding in terms of human common sense and the common good of planet Earth. Though he never uses the term "cosmic fellowship" (which is used by Martin Luther King, Jr.), he thinks in terms of the interconnectedness of Man and Nature. There are multiple examples of this spirit of fellowship and interconnectedness in Gandhi's writings and letters, which invite us to think more about the ways of respecting animals.

Let us not forget that the ecological imperative of Gandhi is also a reflection on his theory of Swaraj as self-rule and self-realization. In a letter to Charlie Andrews dated March 2, 1921, Gandhi spells out the duty of loving animals: "The crime against the untouchables I feel, the exploitation of dumb millions I feel, but I realize still more clearly our duty to the lower animal world. When Buddha carried that lamb on his back and chastised the Brahmins, he showed the highest measure of love."[9] As we can see from Gandhi, the respect for the otherness of the Other in respect to biodiversity is essentially an empathetic exchange with the animality of animals and the plants of plants. That is why Gandhi believed that his service to human beings includes service to the animal world. However, he also knew that it would not be easy to persuade human beings to abstain from practising violence against animals. He proclaimed:

> Though I myself refrain from violence toward animals I must admit that I am not fit enough to dissuade others from it. I know that we have a duty towards animals but cannot make others feel it. For that I need to have far greater purity, compassion and self-control in me. Without these, I cannot have deep spiritual knowledge, and, in the absence of such knowledge, I cannot find the proper language. Without this kind of knowledge, one cannot have self-confidence. I do not believe that I have the strength to persuade others to refrain from violence towards animals [...]. I have surrendered all my powers to Lord Krishna. If, therefore, I ever acquire the strength to stop violence to animals, I will not let it remain unused.[10]

9 Gandhi, Mohandas K., The *Collected Works of Mahatma Gandhi*, Vol. XIX, New Delhi: Publications Division, Ministry of Information and Broadcasting, Government of India, 1925, p. 395.

10 Ibid., Vol. 31, 1925, pp. 474–475.

Gandhi's insistence on empathy and compassion towards animals was a mark of civilisation and moral progress. He asserted: "The moral progress of a nation and its greatness should be judged by the way it treats its animals."[11] He also added: "If someone were to ask me what the most important outward manifestation of Hinduism was, I would suggest that it was the idea of cow protection."[12] In this relation, two incidents in Gandhi's life describe the lack of compassion of human beings to animals. The first incident was in April 1921 and related to driving bullocks. Gandhi wrote:

> Morning broke and I woke up. To my dismay, I found that the driver's goad had a sharpened nail fixed in it and he made the bullocks run by frequently piercing their backs with it. Because of this torture, the bullocks had been shedding liquid excreta all along the route [...]. I requested him to remove the nail from the goad. He promised to do so. Whether he will keep his word or not is a different question. This incident affected me deeply. I realized how thoughtless and devoid of pity our way of life was. Every action of ours ought to be informed with thoughtfulness and compassion and I clearly felt there should be more compassion where there are more weakness, helplessness and dumbness. That we feel sympathy for our own species is nothing to admire particularly. We certainly ought to feel it. But are not cattle even more helpless, miserable and dumb than victims of famine? The famine-stricken, when made desperate by their suffering, may even fight with us, but what can the bullock do? It can neither speak nor rebel. I remembered the dialogue of beasts of the text-book. I felt convinced of the truth of its central idea.[13]

By reading these words of Mahatma Gandhi, one can realize that, as in the case of Lord Buddha, his conception of life has been very different from ours. What might appear strange to a violent techno-scientific civilisation like ours is to be re-educated regarding the concept of life on planet Earth. Gandhi, like Thoreau and Tolstoy, knew well that there is no *Amor Mundi* (love of the world) without friendship and companionship with Nature. This companionship necessitates a level of maturity that is lacking today in the context of any

11 Gandhi, Mohandas K., *Young India*, 1925, p. 160.
12 Gandhi, Mohandas K., *How to Serve the Cow*, Ahmedabad: Navajivan Trust, 1954, pp. 3–4.
13 Gandhi, Mohandas K., Navajivan, April 5, 1921, quoted in Yadav, Yogendra, *Thoughtful Living and Mahatma Gandhi*, https://gandhiking.ning.com/profiles/blogs/thoughtful-living-and-mahatma-gandhi-1.

encounter between Man and Nature. For Gandhi, and not for us, life was a matter of living in truth. Gandhi was very conscious of the fact that the cultivation of an "enlarged pluralism", which includes Nature requires practices where the dimension of all living creatures is taken into account. This indeed is a vision of life with mature and fruitful insights that may help us confront the dilemmas of the twenty-first century: among them, how to create a sense of Earth community, how to turn dialogue with Nature into a moral understanding of the Other natural citizens of Earth democracy, and how to realise the potential of non-violence to heal a torn world of biodiversity.

Gandhi said: "The golden way is to be friends with the world."[14] However, we can only be a friend of the world if we learn to be in dialogue with it. This is how the two concepts of bio-conviviality and enlarged pluralism take on the task of fostering togetherness and solidarity with the Earth. Radical love of the world sits at the centre of radical non-violence, which perseveres through crisis and catastrophe and yields moral integrity. It is a new way of life and a new way of struggle that teaches us to transform our worldwide neighbourhood into a worldwide partnership. The ecological imperative envisions a new way of living that reflects our understanding that the Earth is home not only for humans but for all living species. The ideal life that Gandhi visualised in his village democracies was small and self-sufficient. According to Judith Brown,

> Gandhi's experiments with simple, communal living and with health for villagers, which did not rely on expensive drugs, even led him to consideration of mankind's relations with the environment, human obligations towards animals, and use of air, water and soil [...] his breadth of concern again fed him to ask fundamental questions about life. They make him sound distinctly modern as his ideals of simplicity and smallness of scale echo the fears of people in the later part of the century who have glimpsed some of the darker aspects and unsuspected repercussions of industrialization of the Western civilization he so condemned.[15]

The non-violent call of Nature is to restore the harmony between Man and Nature that has been lost due to the extreme destruction and violence inflicted by man on nature. An egoistic man who has detached himself from nature needs to adhere to the call of Nature. He who can listen to the call of Nature

---

14 Gandhi, Mohandas K., *All Men are Brothers*, edited by Krishna Kripalani, Ahmedabad: Navajivan Publishing House, 1971, p. 191.

15 Brown, Judith M., *Gandhi: Prisoner of Hope,* New Haven and London: Yale University Press, 1989. pp. 393–394.

is closest to the notion of "cosmic fellowship". Thus, the call of Nature is to invoke environmental sustainability, in other words, responsible stewardship of natural resources. The Gandhian notion of ecological sustainability originates from his fundamental ideology of simple living. According to Gandhi, development is associated with the attribute of destruction. Therefore, the material betterment of human life will always commence overexploitation of resources and consequently ecological degradation. The mindless consumption of natural resources has become the reason for the unsustainability of modern civilization.

According to Gandhi, a long-term development process that places the moral responsibility of individuals on their lifestyle, community level, national as well as international levels is considered sustainable development. The non-violent imperatives, according to Gandhi, were embedded in the doctrine of "Sarvodaya", advocated by him and reflected the harmonious existence of humankind with nature and other living beings. In other words, it reflected "ecological sustainability". The notion of "Sarvodaya" reflected "Universal Upliftment" or "Progress of All". The relationship between man and nature should be that of a custodian. Humans serve as custodians of nature and bequeath the natural resources for future generations. When human civilisation views natural resources as curators, individuals would try to restore every part of it for the future. Such a model is referred to as the "Trusteeship" model. The model inculcated the attribute of non-possession in the state, for the individuals and all the stakeholders. All wealth and land are considered common property, to be utilised for the welfare of society. The members owning access to resources will serve as custodians of excess resources and become the trustees of excess wealth. This excess wealth is further used for the uplift of weaker sections of society. Gandhi used the phrase "Economy of Nature," bringing about a sensitivity and deeper understanding of human actions and ecology. Gandhi's every action or thought undertaken was a reflection of minimising wants. The famous Dandi Yatra of 1930 was motivated by the right of the common man over natural resources. Salt, being the primary natural resource, became a significant part of freeing the world from the detrimental greed of materialism.

An environmentally conscious individual will make ethical choices in daily life, such as energy-conserving habits, saving water, and choosing food, clothes, and travel, and so on. The spirit of saving the environment, in turn, will evolve individuals as humans. Gandhi's notion of development involved the emphasis on non-use value and the altruistic value assigned to goods, is a strategic reflection of the missing fundamentals of Gandhian thought in economics.

For the notion of sustainable consumption, Gandhi proposed the ideology of means and ends and distinguished wants from desires. The notion of means and ends holds phenomenal significance in the goal of ecological sustainability. The interconnection between means and ends is more ethical than technical. He emphasised that evil or violent means will never lead to good ends. His notion of means and ends is similar to that of a seed and a tree, signifying the close connection between the two.

One can say that ecological sustainability can only be realised by living day-to-day life most sustainably, and not by fragmenting the pathways independently. Since each of the SDGs is interconnected, the choice of the means to attain the common goal of ecological sustainability is crucial. The more ethical, apolitical, and selfless (devoid of vested interests) the policies or means adopted are, the more chances are that we are drawn closer to the Truth of the goal.

For Gandhi, ecological sustainability calls for the responsibility of human beings to maintain and preserve the interlinkages between man, nature, and other living and non-living entities. It needs the inner transformation of all individuals in society, taking them away from the clutches of greed, selfishness, sense of ownership, and accumulation of wealth. A change in attitude that accommodates all the living and non-living entities in nature, who distinguishes between ethical means and values the importance of means over the ends. According to Gandhi, sustainability is embedded in the day-to-day activities of human life, the way humans consume, produce commodities, and use resources to meet their demands. Every day, the demand created by an individual is a reflection of his level of self-realisation of truth. The means adopted by individuals to meet or achieve that demand is also a reflection of how they conceive the whole philosophy of non-violent existence and "economy of permanence".

For Gandhi, Nature was analogous to God. However, when Nature is not considered God and is understood as limited by Time and Space, then nature could strike through in the future. In this context, human life is said to be Transient compared to that of Nature, which is Permanent. Thus, the notion of an "economy of permanence", based on Gandhian thoughts, was contributed by J. C. Kumarappa (Kumarappa, 1946).[16] This philosophy reinforces the individual to adopt a lifestyle guided by individual responsibility that arises from the essence of the continuity of life. The concept of flow and stock embedded in the philosophy of the "economy of permanence" is a great learning from nature. For attributes of permanence and resilience, nature

16 Kumarappa, Joseph Cornelius, *The Economy of Permanence*, Delhi: Maganvadi, 1946.

teaches us to be a flow, like a river or air. A man must never get stuck at any point in life, an event, a failure, and so on. Sustainability and resilience lie in moving forward, just like a river or air, and not becoming a stock. Thus, in this transient human life, we do not have the right to damage nature that persists and is permanent.

Gandhian notion of ecological sustainability believed in the oneness of life; all creation, both living and non-living, are so closely interdependent that one cannot harm the other without harming oneself. This notion leads us to the concept of Pareto optimality, defined in welfare economics as a state in which resources are optimized in such a manner that any movement away from this state will make at least one person worse off without making any person better off.[17] The notion of Pareto optimality ignored the existence of the environment. In the Gandhian framework, the optimality or harmony is achieved not only within the human, mind and body and among humans, but also between humans and the environment surrounding them. It is the attainment of harmony with universal Truth, the Ultimate Reality, and it is this harmony that sustains through life and beyond life.

Gandhi's notion of sustainability was based on ethical and moral transformation within the individuals themselves. This journey of enlightenment that individuals experience bears the seeds of sustainability. Further, this process of learning and living envisages humanity to strike the balance between lifestyle, nature, and the ultimate Truth. The ashrams of Gandhi are living examples of practical demonstrations of his philosophy. The journey of self-transformation, which is the underlying principle of Gandhian philosophy, travelled both the inner and outer worlds.

The fundamental notion of interconnectedness between every living and non-living entity of nature. This underlying principle of interconnectedness becomes the basis for everyday activity in the community. Every activity is systematically linked to attaining self-transformation and uplift towards ethical and moral values. The activities in the ashrams revolve around sustainable agricultural practices, adopting organic methods of growing vegetables, and conserving resources such as water. All such activities promote and foster individual skills and effectively deploy environmentally sustainable technology, conserving resources.

The Phoenix Settlement in Natal was Gandhi's first experiment with an Ashram in 1904, based on Ruskin's *Unto This Last.* The ashram life advocated a lifestyle that enabled individuals to live in harmony not only with fellow humans but also with nature, thus propagating the notion of ecological

17 https://www.sciencedirect.com/topics/engineering/pareto-optimality.

sustainability. Self-reliance, creativity, and community service were the attributes emphasised by such a living. Such a community propagated collective living, constructive activity, and simple living. The alternative notion thus propagated was not to achieve greater wealth but simpler pleasure. Later, based on Phoenix Settlement, Tolstoy Farm was established in 1910. The preliminary notion behind the establishment of Tolstoy farm was the opportunity to experiment with novel ideas and thoughts.

Gandhi believed that an individual's life was meant for self-realization, which emerges from the search for the "Absolute Truth". The Truth could be realised by the method of "soul force", the use of the permanent and superior nature of the soul. To realise the soul force, certain principles were laid down to accomplish the attainment of Truth or *Satya*. First was the principle of ahimsa, implying non-violence. The second principle was asetya, meaning non-stealing, non-covetousness. The third principle was aparigraha, implying non-possession and non-acquisitiveness, and the fourth principle was brahmacharya, meaning practising celibacy, an attribute emphasised in the Hindu religion as essential for moral growth and uplift. The process of self-realization and self-transformation is a continuous process, and it requires effort each day. Daily life in the ashram must reflect the new order or phenomenon necessary to realise the transformation. A human could tap his or her full potential only by living closer to Nature. The presence of open space, trees, and fruits provided residents with a huge opportunity for farming and gardening. Such activities of farming and gardening engaged all the members with some sort of engagement with nature or the other.

Satyagraha Ashram, also referred as Sabarmati Ashram, was the first Ashram established by Gandhi after he returned to India. Everyone seeking to serve society must be motivated to achieve total detachment. On account of the protest against the mill yarn, the members ceased wearing clothes manufactured by the mill. Many of the women were untouchables; they were encouraged to join the spinning and weaving work at the Ashram. In 1934, Gandhi selected Wardha for Harijan service and the promotion of village industries. In Wardha Ashram, fellow inmates were motivated to take up village work on the same lines as Sabarmati Ashram. Later, Wardha, Central India, was decided as the headquarters. The inmates of the ashram lived a very simple life, performing the daily schedule of the ashram that included prayers, spinning, manual labour, cleaning, and farming. The ashram had a bookshop, a dairy farm, a kitchen that functioned on the biogas plant, and ran a school based on *Nai Talim.*

For Gandhi, the Sevagram ashram was a laboratory of ahimsa. What he experimented on there in the ashram could provide him with a solution to the larger challenges encountered by the nation. Thus, the ashram was run based on constructive activities related to cleanliness, health, education, agricultural innovation, and self-sufficiency in fuel, energy, water, and food. The kitchen, toilets, and premises of the ashram were kept spotless, while the residents cleaned and washed their own utensils. Some of the daily activities were compulsory; for example, daily cleaning the teeth with neem or babul twigs was compulsory. In the beginning, the used twigs were discarded or thrown away. Later, Gandhi recommended that these twigs be collected, washed, dried, and then burnt as fuel. Several day-to-day activities from the ashram life served as a lesson of sustainable living for the human race. The peelings discarded after cutting vegetables were collected and kept under a compost pit. Gandhi insisted that food be eaten raw to conserve fuel. For Gandhi, the economic benefit must be associated with moral and social uplift, as according to him, only material growth or uplift can never be sustainable and would never address the goal of sustainability. The education system developed at Sevagram by Gandhi was referred to as "Basic Education" or "*Nai Talim*". This was an initiative for restructuring the Indian education pattern. Education constitutes the basis of society, and it is an integral factor in building social, political, and economic reforms.

India is home to a large number of people belonging to various racial groups, ethnic groups, cultural backgrounds, and social structures. The tribal societies in remote areas represent an ethnic base of Indigenous communities with their unique patterns of living, originating from nature. The Indigenous knowledge of tribal communities and their best practices for living in harmony with nature have enabled them to predict nature and disasters related to nature to a very large extent. Several indicators are taken into account while predicting nature, such as colour, the direction of flow of clouds, and lightning in the clouds. For instance, if the clouds are rough and small, tossed about by the wind and have the shapes of camels, corms, dead bodies, and monkeys, tribals were able to predict the probability of drought or flood calamities. Most of the tribal regions in India are sacred sites and act as repositories of spiritual and ecological significance. These indigenous traditional tribes are emotionally connected with their ecological surroundings. Their mythological tales reflect a substantial aspect of their life.

The tribals have developed a symbiotic relationship between endowed biological resources and cultural diversities. The tribals even used scientific methods to upgrade the old systems for better hydropower use, such as irrigation of crops and water for drinking. Nutritive crops like barley and buckwheat were cultivated, and approximately twenty crops were grown as staple food. The rotation of farm fields was used for the replenishment of nutrients. Approximately fifteen plant species were found to be used by local people for medicinal purposes to foster a healthcare system. A product known as loofahs, used to remove dead skin, is made from biodegradable and environmentally friendly methods. A hand fan is made of leaves of wine palm, which are dried and cut down. A liquid is extracted after filtering out charcoal bits and ashes called "*chakhwi*", is used to prepare the traditional dish, the liquid extracted after filtering out charcoal bits and ashes called "*chakhwi*", is used to prepare the traditional dish are all products made using best practices from nature.

The consensus-based, decentralised decision-making system adopted by the tribal communities is the most sustainable and peaceful system. It is devoid of the accumulation of wealth, mass consumption, and private ownership and follows the trusteeship model. It ultimately generates a more peaceful, non-violent economy. This system makes the tribal people realise their social and political responsibility, making each person responsible and liable for every act of production and consumption. The usual top-down approach deployed by governments to implement ecologically sustainable policies is inefficient and ineffective. The decisions undertaken by the top-down approach represent the interest of all the members without the full agreement of the community. On the other hand, the consensus-based decision-making system deployed by the tribes delivers a very peaceful, non-violent, and self-sufficient community. It is evident that perceiving ecological sustainability, sustainable consumption patterns, and the conservation of medicinal plants can efficiently be visualised with a decentralised, consensus-based decision-making system.

The non-violent imperatives from such tribal communities are in the form of the best practices of tribal communities in policy formulations that will help achieve Sustainable Development Goal 8, SDG 8, which is to promote sustained, inclusive, and sustainable economic growth. The non-violent appeal from "the real heroes of India", 'the tribals', is to save nature, the animals, and the plants around us. The tribal communities demonstrate and depict the most robust pathways to accomplishing Sustainable Development Goal 13 (SDG 13), which involves taking urgent actions to combat climate change. The best practices adopted by tribals, coupled with their knowledge and skills, would strengthen the sustainable pathways to achieve Sustainable Development Goal 12 (SDG 12). Various awareness programmes can be organized in collaboration with the tribal communities to save and conserve the most useful medicinal plants, which are extremely necessary for health and well-being. Such initiatives will help achieve Sustainable Development Goal 15 (SDG 15). The Sustainable Development Goal SDG 12, which ensures sustainable consumption and production patterns, can be visualized by the consensus-based, decentralised governance system. Thus, one can say that the collective appeal of Sustainable Development Goals is the call of Nature.

Let us not forget that the entire idea of "cosmic fellowship" revolves around the concept of epistemic humility. That is why any form of rapprochement between Man and Nature should be, at the same time, a critique of the epistemological arrogance of modern rationality and its authoritarian practices in terms of colonial thinking and imperialistic domination. As Gandhi argued:

> Where there is egotism, we shall find incivility and arrogance. Where it is absent, we shall find a sense of self-respect together with civility [...] He who holds his self-respect dear acts towards everyone in a spirit of friendship, for he values others' self-respect as much as he values his own. He sees himself in all and everyone else in himself and puts himself in line with others. The egotist keeps aloof from others and, believing himself superior to the rest of the world, he takes [it] upon himself to judge everyone and the result enables the world to have the measure of his smallness.[18]

We can find here the intellectual capacity to engage with the ecological imperatives of our common fate. The urgent appeal to a mature and conscientious political ecology and a nobility of spirit that is open to the call of Nature continues to be the strongest non-violent response to the climate challenges of our time. Maybe that is why green non-violence remains our contemporary ecological battle cry, while it belongs also to our uncertain future.

18 Gandhi, Mahatma, *Selected Political Writings*, edited by Dennis Dalton, Indiana: Hackett Publishing, 1996, pp. 48–49.

BIBLIOGRAPHY

Baber, F. Walter, Bartlett, Robert V., *Deliberative Environmental Politics: Democracy and Ecological Rationality*, Cambridge: The MIT Press, 2005.

Balthrop-Lewis, *Thoreau's Religion: Walden Woods, Social Justice, and the Politics* of *Asceticism*, Cambridge: Cambridge. University Press, 2021.

Chavez-Segura, Alejandro, *A Theology of International Relations: A Buddhist Approach to Religion and Politics in an Interdependent World*, St. Andrews: University of St. Andrews, Dissertation, 2011.

Cooper, David E., James, Simon P., *Buddhism, Virtue and Environment*, London: Routledge, 2017.

Daily, G.C., *Nature's Services: Societal Dependence on Natural Ecosystems,* Washington, DC: Island Press, 1997.

Dale, V.H., Brown, S., Haeuber, R.A. [and others], "Ecological Principles and Guidelines for Managing the Use of Land," *Ecological Applications*, 2000.

Descartes, René, *Discourse on the Method*, translated by Donald A. Cress, Indianapolis: Hackett, 1985.

Dutta, Krishna, Robinson, Andrew, *Rabindranath Tagore: The Myriad Minded Man*, London: Bloomsbury, 1995.

Gandhi, Mahatma, *Quotes of Mahatma Gandhi*, edited by D. Brewer, Wisdom Collection Book, published by Lulu.com, 2020.

Gandhi, Mahatma, *Selected Political Writings*, edited by Dennis Dalton, Indiana: Hackett Publishing, 1996.

Gandhi, Mohandas Karamchand, *All Men are Brothers*, Compiled and edited by Krishna Kripalani, Ahmedabad: Navajivan Publishing House, 1971.

Gandhi, Mohandas Karamchand, *An Autobiography or The Story of My Experiments with Truth*, Ahmedabad: Navajivan, 1948.

Gandhi, Mohandas Karamchand, The *Collected Works of Mahatma Gandhi*, New Delhi: Publications Division, Ministry of Information and Broadcasting, Government of India, 1999.

Gandhi, Mohandas Karamchand, *From Yervada Mandir*, Ahmedabad: Navajivan Publishing, 2007.

Gandhi, Mohandas Karamchand, *Hind Swaraj or Indian Home Rule,* Ahmedabad: Navjivan Publishing, 1938.

Gandhi, Mohandas Karamchand, *How to Serve the Cow*, Ahmedabad: Navajivan Trust, 1954.

Gandhi, Mohandas Karamchand, *India of My Dreams*, Ahmedabad: Navajivan Publishing, 1947.

Gandhi, Mohandas Karamchand, *Panchayat Raj*, Ahmedabad: Navajivan Publishing, 1959.

Gandhi, Mohandas Karamchand, *Truth is God*, compiled by R.K. Prabhu, Ahmedabad: Navajivan Publishing, 1955.

Gandhi, Mohandas Karamchand, *Village Swaraj*, Ahmedabad: Navajivan Publishing, 1962.

Gandhi, Rajmohan, *Mohandas: A True Story of* a *Man, His People, and* an *Empire*, New Delhi: Penguin Books, 2007.

Girardet, H., ed., *Surviving the Century: Facing Climate Chaos and Other Global Challenges*, London: Routledge, 2012.

Jung, Carl Gustav, *Letters*, Vol. 1, edited by G. Adler, Princeton: Princeton University Press, 1975.

Jung, Carl Gustav, *The Visions Seminars*, Zurich: Spring Publications, 1976.

Kaczynski, David, "Why Democracy Needs Dharma," in *Mindful Politics: A Buddhist Guide to Making the World a Better Place*, edited by Melvin McLeod, Boston: Wisdom Publications, 2006.

Kant, Immanuel, *Toward Perpetual Peace and Other Writings on Politics, Peace, and History*, New Haven: Yale University Press, 2008.

Kato, Bunno, Tamura, Yoshiro, *The Threefold Lotus Sutra*, Tokyo: Kosei Publishing, 1989.

Kennington, Richard, "Rene Descartes," in *History of Political Philosophy*, 3rd ed., edited by Leo Strauss and Joseph Cropsey, Chicago: University of Chicago Press, 1987.

Khoshoo, T.N., *Mahatma Gandhi: An Apostle of Applied Human Ecology*, New Delhi: Tata Energy Research Institute, 1995.

Kumarappa, Joseph Cornelius, *The Economy of Permanence*, Delhi: Maganvadi, 1946.

Lubchenco, J., Olson, A.M., Brubaker, L.B. [and others], "The Sustainable Biosphere Initiative: An Ecological Research Agenda," *Ecology*, 1991.

Mandelbaum, D.G., *Society in India: Continuity and Change*, Vol. 1, Berkeley: University of California Press, 1970.

Marcus Aurelius, *Meditations*, Book V/4, London: Penguin Books, 2004.

Miller, Dale E., Eggleston, Ben, *Moral Theory and Climate Change*, London: Routledge, 2020.

Pascal, Blaise, *Pensées*, New York: E.P. Dutton & Co., 1958.

Pearce, David, Markandya, Anil, *The Top 50 Sustainability Books*, London: Routledge, 2017.

Quayum, Mohammad A., *The Poet and His World: Critical Essays on Rabindranath Tagore*, New Delhi: Orient BlackSwan, 2011.

Quayum, Mohammad A., *Rabindranath Tagore: Selected Short Stories*, Introduction, New Delhi: McMillan, 2011.

Qureishi, Naeem M., *Pan-Islam in British Indian Politics: A Study of the Khilafat Movement, 1918–1924*, Leiden: Brill, 1999.

Ramakrishnan, Ram, *Many Paths, One Destination: Love, Peace, Compassion*, Wheatmark: Arizona, 2009.

Schopenhauer, Arthur, *Essays and Aphorisms*, translated by R.J. Hollingdale, London: Penguin Books, 2004.

Tagore, Rabindranath, *A Visit to Japan*, New York: East West Institute, 1961.

Tagore, Rabindranath, "Construction verses Creation," in *Lectures and Addresses*, Madras: Macmillan, 1950.

Tagore, Rabindranath, *Creative Unity*, London: Macmillan, 1962.

Tagore, Rabindranath, *Gitanjali*, Delhi: Macmillan, 1966.
Tagore, Rabindranath, *The Jewel that is Best: Collected Brief Poems*, New Delhi: Penguin Books India, 2011.
Tagore, Rabindranath, *Letters to a Friend: Rabindranath Tagore's Letters to C.F. Andrews*, New Delhi: Rupa, 2002.
Tagore, Rabindranath, *Personality*, Delhi: Macmillan India, 1980.
Tagore, Rabindranath, *The Religion of Man*, Boston: Beacon Press, 1966.
Tagore, Rabindranath, *Sadhana: The Realisation of Life*, London: Filiquarian Publishing, 2006.
Tagore, Rabindranath, The *Sky of Indian History: Themes and Thoughts of Rabindranath Tagore*, Compiled and edited by S. Jeyaseela Stephen, New Delhi: UBS Publishers, 2010.
Tagore, Rabindranath, *Stray Birds*, New York: Macmillan & Co, 1916.
Tagore, Rabindranath, *Towards Universal Man*, New Delhi: Asia Publishing House, 1961.
Tendulkar, D.G., et al., eds., *Gandhiji. His Life and Work*, Bombay: Keshav Bhikaji Dhawale, 1944.
Thomas, Mark, *Gandhi and His Ashrams*, Mumbai, India: Popular Prakashan Pvt. Ltd, 1993.
Thoreau, Henry David, *I to Myself: An Annotated Selection from the Journal of Henry D. Thoreau*, edited by Jeffrey S. Cramer, New Haven: Yale University Press, 2008.
Thoreau, Henry David, *Walden*, Boston: Beacon Press, 1997, 2004.
Thoreau, Henry David, *Walden and Other Writings*, New York: The Modern Library, 2000.
Vettickal, Thomas, *Sarvodaya of Mahatma Gandhi: Realistic Utopia*, Thesis, University of Toronto, 1998.
Vitousek, P.M., Mooney, H.A., Lubchenco, H.A., and Melillo, J.M., "Human Domination of Earth's Ecosystems," *Science*, 1997, 277, pp. 494–499.
Woodcock, George, *Anarchism*, Middlesex: Penguin Books, 1963.

INDEX

www.ingramcontent.com/pod-product-compliance
Ingram Content Group UK Ltd.
Pitfield, Milton Keynes, MK11 3LW, UK
UKHW011939300825
462354UK00005B/21

9 781839 993305